ISBN: 978-0-9894338-1-5
Cover Design: Jenna Stanbrough
Book Layout: Bethany Stanbrough
Front Cover Photos: Spencer Allen and USA Track & Field

Roho Publishing
4040 Graphic Arts Road
Emporia, KS 66801

www.rohopublishing.com

About Roho Publishing

When Kip Keino defeated Jim Ryun in the 1968 Olympic Games at 1500 meters he credited the win to "Roho." Roho is the Swahili word for spirit demonstrated through extraordinary strength and courage. The type of courage and strength that can be summoned up from deep within that will allow you to meet your goals and overcome the challenges in life. Roho Publishing focuses on the spirit of sport and is designed to inspire, encourage, motivate and teach valuable life lessons.

Dedication

To all coaches who work with young people on a daily basis and make a difference. You make a difference in developing not only the physical components, but also the hearts and minds of athletes.

Acknowledgements

Thanks to my parents, who instilled integrity, a strong work ethic, perseverance and pride.

I would like to acknowledge my daughters, Bethany, Leslie and Jenna. Fortunately, Bethany and Jenna majored in journalism and mass media, respectively, and have been an integral part of editing and developing this book.

I want to thank my wonderful wife who has supported me in all my projects. Her support has been an inspiration.

I would like to thank all the coaches I have had over the years who made a difference in my life. I would also like to thank the athletes whom I have had the privilege to coach over the years. Each of these individuals have taught me much about the qualities to be successful in life—good character, integrity, a strong work ethic, dedication, and perseverance.

Introduction

The most important thing in the Olympic Games is not to win but to take part, just as the most important thing in life is not the triumph but the struggle. The essential thing is not to have conquered but to have fought well. – The Olympic Creed

"Motivational Moments in Men's Track and Field" is designed to inspire, encourage, motivate, and teach us valuable life lessons. The stories are written for those who are currently competing, coaching, have participated in track and field, or are simply a track and field or sports fan. The questions at the end of the stories are designed to challenge, teach, and enable you to grow as you apply these principles to athletics and to the bigger game of life.

All of the athletes are ordinary people who used extraordinary desire to accomplish extraordinary things. Each athlete began simply with a dream, which developed into a belief in themselves. They personify the Olympic philosophy – "there are no great people, rather there are great challenges that ordinary people are forced to meet." Their stories offer hope that we can dream and reach beyond our perceived abilities and achieve personal satisfaction.

The stories are rich in history and designed to be read in a few minutes. The stories pay honor to all the young men and women who enter the arena, who make the attempt, and pursue excellence. These stories of great athletes teach us how to eliminate negative thinking, to focus our attention on what is important, and how to overcome obstacles to reach our goals.

Athletes throughout the past century have entered the competitive arena and competed with honor. Although not all athletes are fortunate to catch an Olympic star, all athletes can valiantly reach for the heavens. Their stories of inspiration should be read and remembered. For it has been written, *"The honor should not alone go to those who have not fallen; rather all honor to those who fall and rise again."*

This book was designed to be enjoyed by anyone with an interest in track and field, but the author, who has over thirty years of experience in coaching track and field at both the high school and collegiate level, wrote this book especially with track and field coaches in mind. If you are a coach, you are encouraged to use these stories to motivate and inspire your athletes. Coaching is one of the most influential professions in our society. Coaches work with young people on a daily basis and have a tremendous opportunity to make a difference. Athletics is about more than just playing a game. It is the responsibility of the coach to develop not only the physical component, but to develop the heart and mind of each athlete they coach.

Our young people need strong role models. The athletes profiled display the drive, motivation, and dedication to train for years to reach a goal. Their stories teach the values of self-discipline, responsibility, accountability, and loyalty. They demonstrate the qualities necessary to be successful in life—good character, integrity, a strong work ethic, dedication, and perseverance.

You're bound to find motivation and encouragement, no matter what your experience or relationship to track and field. Hopefully you receive pleasure and inspiration from these pages, just as you have found pleasure and inspiration from the greatest sport in the world—track and field.

Using the Questions in a Coaching Environment

The short stories are designed to be read in a few minutes and can be posted on bulletin boards or distributed for group discussions. The questions at the end of each story are designed to inspire thinking, encourage, challenge and impart a learning lesson.

The principles embedded in the stories can be applied to athletics, but more importantly to the bigger game of life. Rather than hoping athletes can be gaining positive lessons from the athletic experience, the coach can be proactive by educating athletes through a story and its applications to athletics and life.

There are many ways the questions can be used with an athletic team. Here are ten suggestions.

1. Post on bulletin board for all to read.

2. Distribute event specific stories to athletes.

3. Coach reads story and then a group discussion takes place.

4. Athletes are assigned to read stories to team. Group discussion takes place after story is read.

5. Athletes read story within small group. Small group discussion takes place after story is read.

6. Team discusses questions during warm-up activity or drill.

7. Stories can be read during a break in practice.

8. Questions can be discussed during a break in practice.

9. Reading of story and discussion on stories can take place after practice.

10. Athletes can be given a story to help motivate them when injured or performance is sub-par.

Sample questions from Buddy Edelen story:

1. Buddy Edelen wanted to run with the best, so he moved to where the competition was. Do you enjoy competing against great competition? How can good competition make you better?

2. Despite having a large lead in the Olympic Marathon Trials and suffering because of the heat, Buddy refused to back off and cruise in. What does it mean to run hard, but also run smart?

3. Buddy was a pioneer that helped set the stage for future runners such as gold medal marathoner Frank Shorter. How will you set the stage for athletes to come after you?

Index

Index

Page	Last Name	First Name	Event	Story Overview
62	Redmond	Derek	Sprints	Pulled hamstring in 400-meter Olympic final, limped home with help from his dad
63	Richards	Bob	Multi-Events	Overcame injuries to become two time Olympic pole vault champion
64	Rono	Henry	Distance	Set four world records one summer, overcame alcoholism and being homeless
65	Ryun	Jim	Distance	Known for his grueling workouts; became first high school athlete to break four minutes for the mile
66	Salazar	Alberto	Distance	Known for his running toughness; made his mark as a marathoner
67	Saneyev	Viktor	Jumps	Advocate for drug free athletics, during a time drug use was rampant in his country
68	Santee	Wes	Distance	Sacrificed an opportunity to break the 4 minute mile by helping his collegiate team
69	Scott	Steve	Distance	Ran 136 sub 4 minute miles, which is the most in history
70	Schull	Bob	Distance	Nearly died from asthma as a youth
71	Seagren	Bob	Jumps	Overcame injuries and equipment controversies to medal twice at the Olympics
72	Shay	Ryan	Distance	Promising young runner who died during the Olympic Marathon Trials
73	Sheppard	Mel	Distance	Rejected by the New York Police because of weak heart, but was strong enough to win Olympic gold
74	Shorter	Frank	Distance	Denied Olympic glory when an imposter jumped into the marathon finish
75	Smith	Christian	Distance	Big underdog who dove across the finish line to make the Olympic team
76	Smith	Tommie	Sprints	Participated in a civil rights demonstration that led to punishment, but later was recognized as a hero
77	Stones	Dwight	Jumps	Won 19 national championships but failed to win at the Olympics
78	Taylor	John	Mid-Distance	First great African American role model in track and field
79	Thorpe	Jim	Multi-Events	Difficult childhood, won Olympic gold, before having it stripped and later restored
80	Viren	Lasse	Distance	Was tripped in Olympic 10,000 meters, but got up to win and set world record
81	Warmerdam	Cornelius	Jumps	Broke 15 foot barrier in pole vault using a bamboo pole
82	Whitfield	Mal	Distance	Tailgunner during Korean War, trained on military runways before setting world records
83	Wohluter	Rick	Distance	After he was tripped at the Olympics, he used as motivation to medal at the next Olympic Games
84	Woodruff	John	Distance	African American who overcame Hitler's propaganda and a tactical racing error to win gold
85	Wottle	Dave	Distance	Ran an even pace to surprise the field to win 800 meters Olympic gold
86	Young	Kevin	Hurdles	Made innovative changes to his stride pattern that led to world record at the Olympics
87	Zamperini	Louis	Distance	Military plane shot down, survived 47 days on raft in Pacific and 2.5 years in prison camp
88	Zatopek	Emil	Distance	Known for creating interval training; he relied on determination to become a running legend
89	Zelezny	Jan	Throws	Lost the Olympic gold on the last throw of the competition

John Stephen Akhwari

Never, Never Give Up

One of the most prestigious track and field events in the Olympic Games is the marathon, an event that requires high levels of endurance and courage. In the 1968 Olympic marathon, held at the high altitude of Mexico City, it was not the winner who was best remembered, but the runner who finished last.

The Olympic gold medal was won by Mamo Wolde of Ethiopia. The marathon medals had already been handed out at the awards ceremony earlier. Since the marathon was the last event on the last day, the closing ceremonies had just been completed. Darkness was falling and the spectators and athletes were gathering their belongings to leave the stadium. With just a few thousand spectators left, the announcer asked them to remain in their seats. They could see motorcycles with flashing blue lights, escorting someone into the stadium. Out of the darkness, John Stephen Akhwari, wearing the colors of Tanzania, entered at the far end of the stadium, painfully hobbling, his leg bloody and bandaged. He had taken a terrible fall early in the race at the 2 kilometer mark, banged his head, hurt his knee, and was trampled before he could get back on his feet. Now 40 kilometers later, he was stumbling his way to the finish line. Grimacing with every step, he painfully hobbled one lap around the 400-meter track. The crowd responded and started to cheer, with the ovation getting louder and louder. They encouraged John down the straightaway of his race with a thundering ovation that exceeded the one given to Wolde hours earlier. After a long and torturous lap, John eventually crossed the finish line and collapsed.

The next day, John appeared before reporters and was asked, "Why, after sustaining the kinds of injuries you did, would you ever get up and proceed to the finish line, when there was no way you could possibly place in the race?" John said this, "My country did not send me over 7,000 miles to start a race. They sent me over 7,000 miles to finish one."

John Stephen Akhwari never won an Olympic medal. Yet, he is remembered as the runner whose determination and perseverance represents the true character of a champion.

Questions for Thought:

1. Have you ever thought of quitting anything? Are you prepared to persevere through challenges you encounter on your way to accomplishing a goal?

2. Life is like a marathon, it's a long journey. When you have hope, you are excited about the future. How hopeful of a person are you? What gives you hope?

3. Anyone can begin something, but it is more difficult to finish what you start. How important is it to you to be known as the type of person who finishes what they start?

Horace Ashenfelter

FBI Man

Horace (Nip) Ashenfelter was born in Collegeville, Pennsylvania, and competed in many sports in high school, but never competed in track. After high school, he attended Penn State University. He had his collegiate career interrupted by service as an Army Air Corps fighter pilot during World War II. Following his service career, he returned to Penn State to win a national championship in the two-mile and helped his relay team to a Penn Relays 4x1600-meter relay victory, running with his two brothers on the team.

After graduating from college, Horace won the 1952 Olympic Trials 3000-meter steeplechase, running 9:06.04 to beat a 16-year-old record. At the 1952 Olympics in Helsinki, he was reunited with his collegiate coach, Chick Werner, who was the Olympic coach. Horace lowered his American record in the qualifying heats and in an exciting final, he dueled a Russian competitor to win in 8:45.4, a new world record. He is the only American to hold the steeplechase world record and to win gold in the event. The victory drew much press because the Cold War was in progress. Horace, at the time of his victory, was an FBI agent. The fact that he ran down a Russian made for sensational headlines. However, on the track Horace and the Russians embraced, becoming friends through competition.

Horace qualified again for the 1956 Olympics in Melbourne, Australia, but could only finish sixth in a qualifying heat and failed to make the final.

Horace Ashenfelter demonstrated remarkable versatility in his career by capturing 17 national titles in track and cross country. He remains the only American to ever win an Olympic gold medal in the steeplechase.

Questions for Thought:

1. Horace had his running career interrupted by a war. How would you react if your career was suddenly interrupted?

2. How would you get your career back on track after a long break?

3. Horace became friends with his Russian competitors. How can you build friendships with your competitors?

Charles Austin

Winning The Mental Game

Photo Courtesy of USATF

Charles Austin was raised as the youngest of 10 children in Van Vleck, Texas. Growing up without a father, he watched as his mother struggled to support their family and learned early in his life the importance of a strong work ethic. He did not start his track career until he was a senior in high school, when friends convinced him to try high jumping. He cleared 6-0 on his first try and finished the year with a personal best of 6-11, but he never qualified for the Texas state meet.

Charles' success earned him an athletic scholarship at Southwest Texas University. Although he struggled the first few years, he persisted and achieved great success his senior year, shattering school records and winning the NCAA Outdoor Championships. He won the 1991 World Championships and was a contender to win in the 1992 Olympics. However, he suffered a knee injury, and it adversely affected his confidence and cost him a chance to win a medal.

It was difficult for Charles to watch his fellow competitors compete for the gold. The knee trouble persisted, and he was told he would never jump again unless he had major surgery. While his knee was healing, his passion continued to grow. He began his journey back to the top of the high jump rankings.

Charles began to focus on the 1996 Olympics in Atlanta, with a renewed determination and positive mental attitude. The Olympic high jump final came down to a dramatic finish between Poland's Artur Partyka and Charles of the United States. Partyka cleared 7-9¼ while Austin missed twice at that height. Down to one remaining jump, Charles strategically passed his last attempt at 7-9¼. The bar was moved to 7-10 and Charles had only one attempt remaining. Charles ran his approach with increasing speed, planted, and rose into the air, clearing the bar and taking the lead. Partyka missed at 7-10, and strategically passed to 7-10¾. After two more misses by Partyka, Charles was the Olympic champion with a new Olympic record and American record.

Despite a late start in track and field and a knee injury that threatened to end his career, Charles Austin won an Olympic gold medal and became the American and Olympic high jump record holder, two-time world champion, and a nine-time U.S. national track and field high jump champion.

Questions for Thought:

1. Charles did not rely on luck; he worked hard. How much of athletic success is being lucky?

2. Charles was blessed with physical ability and once he began to focus, he was able to make the most of it. How can you make the most of the physical ability you have been given?

3. Charles believes the mental game is important. How much of athletic success is mental? How much time do you spend developing yourself mentally?

Roger Bannister

Breaking Through Barriers

Running a 4:00 mile was once deemed impossible. Experts said it was unreachable and dangerous to the health of any athlete who attempted to reach it. Roger Bannister of Great Britain was a 25-year-old medical student at Oxford University completing his internship and putting in long hours at the hospital. His workouts were conducted each day during his 30 minute lunch break. He had been expected to win the 1500 meters at the 1952 Olympics, but Roger was jostled during the race, and never got into contention, finishing fourth.

On May 6, 1954, Roger was scheduled to run at Oxford University's track meet. He had stayed up all night doing his medical rounds and didn't feel like running. But he knew his competitors were closing in on the chase to be the first to run a sub-4:00 mile. He had to go for it! He was paced by a pair of "rabbits," clocking 1:58.2 for the first half-mile. His three-quarter mile time was 3:00.5. With 300 meters to go, Roger said he urged himself "to a supreme effort." He crossed the finish line and began sagging to the ground, drained of all his energy. "It was only then that real pain overtook me," he said. "I felt like an exploded flashlight with no will to live; I just went on existing in the most passive physical state without being unconscious."

The crowd that had urged him on fell silent. Two track officials held him up while spectators converged on him. His time was announced. "Three ... "The rest was drowned out by the cheers. Roger's time of 3:59.4 broke the world record and broke the sub-4:00 barrier, but more importantly, it broke the psychological barrier. What was once deemed impossible had been accomplished. Two years later, 16 runners had logged sub-4:00 miles, accomplishing the one task few thought possible.

Questions for Thought:

1. Roger Bannister's claim to fame was being the first to break the four-minute mile; however, the true significance was breaking through a barrier. What is the significance behind Roger's achievement?

2. Within two years after Roger Bannister broke the 4:00 barrier, 16 people had broken 4:00. Since then, over 1300 people have done so. How can something once thought impossible be achieved by so many people?

3. Think about a barrier that limits you. What can you do to break through the barrier?

Bob Beamon

The Man Who Could Fly

Bob Beamon survived a difficult childhood, as his mother died at age 25 from tuberculosis when Bob was less than a year old. Because his father was in prison, Bob was raised by his grandmother, Bessie. Growing up without a father in a tough neighborhood with violence, gangs, and drugs was challenging, and as a young boy his craving for attention made him a troublemaker in school. Bob struck a teacher, was expelled from school, and sent to an alternative school for delinquents in New York. It was there that Bob realized he could make something of his life and he began to use sports as a means of focusing his attention toward positive goals.

Bob established many school and state records as well as a national record in the triple jump while in high school. Bob attended the University of Texas El Paso (UTEP) and worked on his speed and on a long jumping technique called the hitch kick, where the long jumper runs in the air before landing. He won the NCAA Indoor long jump and triple jump and by age 22, Bob was emerging as one of the top jumpers in the world and was in contention to win an Olympic gold medal in the long jump.

Four months before the Olympic Trials in 1968, Bob was suspended from the UTEP track team and lost his athletic scholarship for participating with other blacks in a boycott of a meet against Brigham Young, a Mormon school whose racial policies disturbed them. The suspension meant that Bob was without a coach. Despite the difficulties he was having at UTEP, Bob won the Olympic Trials long jump, and with the exception of one meet, was undefeated that season. Bob was headed to the 1968 Mexico City Olympic Games as a favorite to win the gold medal, but nobody expected what was about to happen.

Bob accelerated down the long jump runway in the thin air of Mexico City. On each of his 19 strides, he continued to build speed. He hit the board perfectly, exploded off the take-off board to a height of 6-0, ran in the air with his hitch kick, and stretched out his legs to land in the sand pit. Not only was he the first long jumper in history to jump 28-0, he also became the first to reach 29-0, shattering the world record by jumping an unbelievable 29-2½. Of all Olympic records, track and field experts consider none as impressive as the one Bob stunningly set in Mexico City.

Bob Beamon overcame adversity as a child to achieve one of the greatest performances in athletic history at the 1968 Mexico City Olympics. In the world of athletics, a tremendous performance is sometimes referred to as "Beamonesque," a tribute to Bob's outstanding long jump.

Questions for Thought:

1. How did adversity help Bob Beamon achieve success?

2. What limits you in achieving what many may think is impossible?

3. When you get a second chance, how can you make the most of it?

Abebe Bikila

The Barefoot Runner

Abebe Bikila was born in Ethiopia, the son of a shepherd. As a young man, Abebe decided to join the Imperial Bodyguard to support his family and walked more than 100 miles to the city of Addis Ababa. Abebe qualified for the Ethiopian Olympic team in the 1960 Olympics held in Rome. He grew up in the plains of Ethiopia running barefoot, and that's how he ran in the Olympics. Abebe shocked the world by winning the marathon in a record time of 2:15:16 and became the first African to win an Olympic gold medal. He opened the door for Africans, primarily Ethiopians and Kenyans, to start dominating distance running.

Abebe returned to Ethiopia as a hero. Emperor Haile Selassie promoted him to the rank of corporal position and awarded him the Star of Ethiopia. However, a revolution occurred and Abebe, who didn't understand politics, was forced to take part, but refused to kill dignitaries. When the revolution failed, all those involved were sentenced to death by hanging. Abebe was placed in prison, where he stayed for months, often being beaten, and it appeared he would be hung. However, his supporters finally convinced officials that Abebe had been unfairly charged and imprisoned.

Shortly before the 1964 Olympics in Tokyo, Abebe had an acute appendicitis. He was told he would not be able to participate in the Olympics and would therefore be unable to defend his marathon title. Not to be denied, he snuck out and started jogging in the hospital courtyard at night. He not only competed (this time wearing shoes), but won again in a record time of 2:12:11, becoming the first athlete in history to win the Olympic marathon twice. Abebe was a hero in Ethiopia and received a car, which was a real status symbol, since there were not many cars in Ethiopia at that time. Ironically, a car accident left him a paraplegic. At the age of 41, the legendary Abebe Bikila's life came to a tragic end when he died of complications from the car accident.

Questions for Thought:

1. Abebe grew up without shoes but overcame that to be an Olympic champion. What obstacles have you overcome to be successful?

2. Despite being a paraplegic, Abebe remained a positive influence on other people. How can you be a positive influence on people even when things are not going right for you?

3. Abebe became the first African to ever win an Olympic Gold medal. He started a longstanding tradition of Africans dominating the distance events. What type of tradition could you start?

Mike Boit

Olympic Opportunity Denied Twice

Mike Boit grew up in the Rift Valley of Kenya and attended St. Patrick's High School, a school well-known for producing world class distance runners. He won the Kenya national high school title in the 800 meters. His first international competition came in his first Olympic Games, the 1972 Olympics in Munich. The Olympic Games were interrupted by tragedy when Palestinian terrorists murdered 11 Israeli athletes and coaches. This was Mike's first trip away from home, and the massacres had a heavy effect on him, as the Kenyans were housed near the Israeli Olympic team. Mike wanted to go home, but was able to regain his focus for the 800 meters final. He put himself in position to win coming off the final curve; however, the U.S. champion Dave Wottle put on a furious kick, coming from last place to win the gold, with Mike medaling in third place. He also came back to finish fourth in the 1500 meters.

The track coach at Eastern New Mexico University, Bill Siverberg, recruited Mike on a trip to Kenya, and he went on to have a standout career for the school, winning two NAIA cross country titles. He set his sights on becoming one of the world's top middle distance runners. He consistently won medals against world championship caliber competition and challenged top runners, often pushing them to world records. As the 1976 Olympics in Montreal approached, Mike was in the prime of his career and poised to go after a gold medal. Unfortunately, he never got the chance to prove he was among the best at an Olympic venue. Kenya boycotted the 1976 Olympics in Montreal after New Zealand broke a world boycott of South Africa's apartheid regime and participated in a rugby competition. Mike's Olympic dream was shattered and he had to wait four more years for an Olympic opportunity.

After four more years of hard training, Mike was ready to prove he was one of the best runners in the world. However, the United States led a boycott of the 1980 Olympics in Moscow, protesting Russia's invasion of Afghanistan, and Kenya joined the boycott. Mike's Olympic dream was shattered once more.

Due to politics, one of the best runners in the world was twice denied an opportunity to win Olympic gold. Mike continued to run competitively, posting a mile best of 3:49.5 and became successful at masters events. He obtained a doctorate degree from the University of Oregon and returned to Kenya to promote running as the Kenya sports commissioner.

Questions for Thought:

1. In Mike's first Olympics, several athletes were murdered and he had to regain his focus. How do you regain your focus when you have been distracted?

2. If you were not able to follow through and have a chance to achieve your goals, how would you feel?

3. What have you learned from adversity that will help you as you strive to live a successful life?

Valery Brumel

Enduring 29 Operations to Come Back

Valery Brumel began training in sports at age 12. By the age of 16, he had jumped 6-6¾. As an 18-year-old, Valery made the Soviet Union Olympic team and entered the 1960 Rome Olympics as a talented but relatively unknown athlete. The competition boiled down to the final two competitors, Robert Shavlakadze and Valery, both from the Soviet Union. Both cleared the same height of 7-1, but Valery had more attempts and had to settle for the silver medal.

Over the next three years, he broke the high jump world record six times, increasing it to 7-5¾. He entered the 1964 Olympic Games as the favorite and improved upon his silver medal of the previous Olympics by winning the gold medal.

After an undefeated 1965 season, tragedy struck when Valery was severely injured in a motorcycle accident. His injuries left him unable to jump, but his love for the sport and competition still remained. Despite 29 operations, Valery would not give up and retained his burning desire to continue high jumping.

Through dedication, perseverance, and hard work he willed his way back to jumping. Gradually, he grew stronger and stronger. Doctors had told him he would never jump again, but Valery defied the odds. He returned to high jumping and jumped 6-9 in his comeback. Unfortunately, he could never get back to the heights he had jumped earlier in his career.

Questions for Thought:

1. Valery overcame 29 operations so that he could return to the sport he loved. How deep is your love for what you do?

2. Have you ever quit an activity because you were out of your comfort zone? Using Valery's story as motivation, how could you work through the discomfort?

3. On a scale of 1-10 (10 is high), how would you rate your perseverance? What could you do to improve your perseverance?

Sergey Bubka

Olympic Curse

As a youth track and field athlete, Sergey Bubka found early success in the 100-meter dash and the long jump. However, when he turned to the pole vault, he became a world-class competitor. His international career started in 1983, when as a virtual unknown he won the world championship in Helsinki, Finland. The following year he set his first world record of 19-2. The Soviet sports system rewarded athletes for setting new world records, and he became noted for establishing new records by slim amounts. As a result of this strategy, Sergey was often jumping at meets to establish a new world record. This made Sergey a big attraction at track and field meets and he often collected bonus payments for new world records.

Sergey is widely regarded as a living legend of sport, building his career into one of the most remarkable dominations sport has ever seen. He held the title of world champion for 16 years (1983 to 1999), won six consecutive gold medals, and is still the only athlete in any event to win six world championships.

Though Sergey completely dominated pole vaulting in his time, he was highly unlucky in the Olympic Games. In 1984, he was the world champion and the favorite to win Olympic gold; however, the USSR, along with the other Eastern Bloc countries, boycotted the 1984 Summer Olympic Games, denying Sergey an opportunity to win his first gold medal. Motivated to prove he was the best pole vaulter in the world, he became the first vaulter in history to clear the previously thought unattainable barrier of 6 meters (19-8¾) in 1985.

Finally, Sergey got to compete in his first Olympic Games in 1988. At the 1988 Seoul Olympics he won the gold medal. Late in the competition, Sergey had two misses, and a third miss at 19-4¼ would mean the world's best pole vaulter would not even medal. Fortunately, Sergey cleared the height and won the long awaited Olympic gold medal with an Olympic record. In 1991 he was the first man to clear 20-0.

Four years later at the 1992 Olympic Games, he was the overwhelming favorite to win, when he failed to clear his first three attempts and was out of the Barcelona Olympics. He set his personal record 20-1¾ in 1994 and entered the Atlanta Olympics in 1996 as a favorite. Sergey's unlucky streak at the Olympic Games continued when he had to withdraw because of a heel injury before he could even take one jump.

Questions for Thought:

1. Sergey Bubka was the most dominant pole vaulter in the world for 16 years. What are the qualities that one must have in order to be good for that long?

2. Despite being the top vaulter in the world for 16 years, Sergey only won one Olympic Games. Did his success at the Olympics define his career? Why or why not?

3. Experts felt a 20-0 pole vault clearance was impossible, but Sergey proved them wrong. Have you ever been told you couldn't achieve something? How did you overcome the barriers?

John Carlos

The Courage to Stand Up For What You Believe

John Carlos was born in Harlem, New York. John learned to fight his way in and out of trouble as a teenager. He originally wanted to be an Olympic swimmer until he realized the training facilities he needed were only for whites or the wealthy only. For John, running came naturally. He was also encouraged to perform well academically and athletically by community minded mentors, whom he credited for keeping him focused, out of trouble, and laying the foundation for his drive to achieve and succeed.

After high school, he attended East Texas State University for one year before transferring to San Jose State University. At San Jose State he led the team to its first NCAA championship in 1969, winning the 100 yards, 220 yards, and the 4x110-yard relay.

In the 1968 200-meter Olympic final in Mexico City, Tommie Smith of the U.S. blazed home in a world record time of 19.83 and John was third. What John and Smith did at the awards ceremony would make history forever. They climbed onto the podium, and as the Star Spangled Banner played, John wore a black glove on his left hand; Smith wore a black glove on his right hand. John's left hand demonstration was meant to represent unity in Black America. Smith's glove on his right hand was meant to represent Black Power in America. The black socks that both wore (and no shoes) represented black poverty in America.

The actions were considered disrespectful and resulted in both men being immediately kicked off the U.S. team. Although the two were considered unpatriotic by many and received death threats, the African-American community greeted them as heroes.

After the Olympics, John persevered to make a difference for the future of all people. Eventually, John Carlos would be recognized as a hero for standing up for civil rights during the 1968 Olympics.

Questions for Thought:

1. John took a stand for what he believed in. What do you stand for?

2. John is now considered a hero. What makes a hero?

3. John credits others with laying the foundation for his success. What goes into laying a foundation for success? Who helps you lay the foundation?

Ron Clarke

Great, but no Medal

At the age of 19, Ron Clarke was a promising young Australian runner who was selected to carry the Olympic flame into the Stadium for the 1956 Olympic Games in Melbourne, Australia. As he carried the torch, his arms got singed. That may have been a premonition, as every time he appeared at an Olympic Games he got burnt, in one way or another. At the time, he was the world junior mile record holder, but a period of national army service prevented him from being selected to the 1956 Australian Olympic team.

Lacking a fierce ambition to be a champion, Ron gave up competition for several years before taking running seriously again. He entered the 1964 Tokyo Olympics as one of the favorites, but he was out-sprinted by the unknown American, Billy Mills, and finished third in the 10,000 meters.

In the 1968 Olympics, Ron's medal ambitions were shattered in the thin air of high altitude Mexico City. Despite training in the Alps to get acclimated to high altitudes at Mexico City, that did not put him on par with his opponents from African countries, whom had always run at high altitude. He ran out of oxygen late in the 10,000 meters, but staggered on bravely, virtually unconscious, to finish sixth. He collapsed on the line and suffered heart damage, which caused him to be required to take daily medication the rest of his life. Ron finished in sixth place, but remembered nothing of the last lap. He sufficiently recovered to compete in the 5000 meters a few days later to finish fifth.

The Olympics were not kind to an athlete who history confirms was an all-time great and the finest distance runner of his time. He set 18 world records, six of them over the Olympic distances of 5000 and 10,000 meters. At one stage, he held every world record from two miles to 20 kilometers.

Ron's magnificence on the track never translated to Olympic gold. Most of his career he was self-coached, and he felt he ran poor tactical races at the Olympic Games.

Questions for Thought:

1. Ron Clarke was one of the greatest distance runners ever, but never won an Olympic gold medal. Is success defined by winning? Why or why not?

2. Ron admits that he may have run better tactical races with a coach. How can you work with someone, such as a coach, to perform better?

3. Ron held 18 world records, but did not win an Olympic championship. Which would you rather have, a record or a big championship? Why?

Sebastian Coe

Double Gold

Sebastian Coe always loved to run. When his father realized that Sebastian had great running potential, he became his coach, although he did not have experience in coaching or running. He talked with people who knew about running, and read all he could find on the subject. He kept Sebastian's mileage low, concentrating on speed and hill training as well as a specialized exercise circuit.

Sebastian quickly improved and in 1979 he set three world records in 41 days. He set his first world record in the 800-meter run (1:42.33), then broke the mile world record (3:48.95) and later, the 1500 meter world record (3:32.03). He remained undefeated at all distances that year, was voted "athlete of the year," and was ranked number one in the world at 800 meters and 1500 meters. Sebastian arrived at the 1980 Moscow Olympics as the world record holder and favorite in the 800 meters. His major competitor was fellow Great Britain countryman, Steve Ovett, who was the favorite to win the 1500 meters because he had not lost in his last 45 races at that distance.

In the 800 meters, Sebastian stayed at the back of the pack, counting on his strong finish. However, he was too far behind and couldn't catch Ovett, settling for the silver. He ran what he called "the worst race" of his life. Sebastian and his father decided that in the upcoming 1500 meters he would run from near the front. In the 1500 meters, the pace was slow, which played into his hands. After running in second most of the race, he surged on the last lap, running 52.2 for the last 400 meters to win the gold.

The rivalry between the two best middle distance runners in the world continued to grow with enormous pressure building on Sebastian and Ovett. They avoided running in the same races for the next four years. Sebastian traded world record mile times back and forth with Ovett. The year before the 1984 Olympics, Sebastian spent most of the year battling health problems and spent several months in and out of the hospital. However, he recovered in time to qualify for the British team in both the 800 and 1500 meters. To the surprise of many, he won another silver medal in the 800 meters behind Joaquim Cruz of Brazil.

In the 1500 meters, Sebastian sprinted into the lead in the final turn and pulled away from Cram to win in an Olympic record of 3:32.53. Coe, unable to win his best event, the 800 meters, in two consecutive Olympics, rose to the occasion to capture the 1500-meter run in two successive Olympic Games. He would later go on to become the head of the London Olympic Committee of the 2012 Olympic Games.

Questions for Thought:

1. Sebastian was unable to win his favorite event, yet moved up to another event and won. If you have multiple events, do you have confidence in your least favorite event?

2. Sebastian changed his tactics from what felt comfortable to what set him up for success. How much courage does it take to get out of your comfort zone to compete?

3. The Coe-Ovett rivalry was one of the greatest in history. Do you have a rival? How do you handle the pressure of competing against your rival?

Harold Connolly

Overcoming a 'Hand'icap

Harold "Hal" Connolly competed in four Olympics Games as a United States hammer thrower, broke the world record six times, and held the world record for almost 10 years in an event in which Americans seldom do well. When Hal won the Olympic Gold medal in 1956 at the Melbourne Olympic Games, photographers yelled at him to raise his arms in triumph. He lifted his right arm only because he could not lift his left. Hal's left arm was injured during birth, and he fractured it 13 times as a child. His left arm grew to be four and a half inches shorter than his right and his left hand two-thirds the size of his right.

Hal wanted to be normal. In his memoir he stated, "I wanted to push myself into the 'normal' society. I was a handicapped person who knows the agony of all-out trying and not accomplishing."

Hal was not recruited out of high school, and he paid his own way to Boston College, where he was a mediocre shot-putter. One day, he was retrieving hammers for the hammer throwers in practice and he was throwing them back farther than the hammer throwers had thrown them. He was quickly switched from the shot put to the hammer throw. The hammer is a 16-pound metal ball attached to a handle by a wire almost four feet long. The thrower spins three or four times in a ring before releasing. What Hal lacked in arm strength, he made up for with speed and leg power.

Hal won 12 national titles, including nine in the hammer outdoors and three indoors with the 35-pound weight throw. By 1955, he was the first American to surpass 200-0, throwing 201-5. That was just the beginning of his record-setting exploits. He earned his first world record with a throw of 224-10 shortly before the 1956 Olympics. Wearing ballet shoes to improve his footing in the concrete ring, he beat long-time world record holder Mikhail Krivonosov to win the Olympic gold medal.

After his gold medal, Hal competed in three more Olympics. He finished eighth in 1960, sixth in 1964 and failed to qualify for the finals in 1968. He retired as a teacher and served 11 years as the executive director of the Special Olympics. Until his death, he coached young athletes and served as the Junior Hammer Development Chairmen for the U.S.A. Track and Field. Hal was one of the leading promoters for the next generation of hammer throwers.

Question for Thought:

1. Hal didn't let his handicap affect him. In fact, it motivated him to work harder. How would a handicap motivate you to work harder?

2. Hal switched to a different event in college. Are you willing to try new things?

3. How do you promote your event?

Glenn Cunningham

The Iron Man From Kansas

Photo courtesy of Kansas Athletics

When he was 7 years old, Glenn and his older brother Floyd had the chore of starting a fire in the rural schoolhouse stove every cold morning. One February morning in 1916, the kerosene container had accidentally been filled with gasoline. The stove exploded and both Glenn and Floyd were terribly burned. There was no phone and no ambulance, so they ran two miles home before receiving treatment. Floyd died, and Glenn's legs were so badly burned, his doctors told him he would never walk again. He was bed-ridden for months. Showing a fierce determination and with a great deal of agony, he slowly began to recover and was able to walk on crutches. Finally, he got rid of the crutches but, as he said later, "It hurt like thunder to walk, but it didn't hurt at all when I ran. So for five or six years, about all I did was run."

Glenn became a miler in high school in Elkhart, Kansas, and set a high school record of 4:24.7 in his last race. He entered the University of Kansas in 1931 and won the NCAA 1500-meter title in 1932. Glenn went on to finish fourth in the 1932 Olympic 1500 meters. In the 1936 Olympic Games in Berlin, he put on a burst of speed in the third lap to try to break away from the field, but took a silver medal behind New Zealand's Jack Lovelock, who ran a world record 3:47.8.

Because of circulation problems caused by his childhood accident, Glenn needed nearly an hour to prepare for a race. He first had to massage his legs and he then required a long warm-up period. He overcame the odds and was the fastest American miler during the 1930's, setting a world record in 1934 of 4:06.8, and also an 800-meter world record of 1:49.7.

Questions for Thought:

1. How did Glenn Cunningham overcome his adversity?

2. Think of an adversity that you have had. How did you overcome it?

3. What do you think is the most important factor in overcoming a challenge?

Cliff Cushman

I Dare You!

Photo courtesy of Kansas Athletics

Cliff Cushman was a remarkably versatile athlete whose talents ranged from a 4:11.6 mile to a sixth place finish in the NCAA triple jump. While attending the University of Kansas, Cliff won the 400-meter hurdles at the 1960 NCAA Championships. He went on to make the U.S. Olympic Team and won a silver medal in the 1960 Olympic Games in Rome in the 400-meter hurdles. He was voted the North Dakota athlete of the year in 1960. Cliff trained hard as he pursued his dream of capturing a gold medal at the 1964 Olympic Games in Tokyo. In the 1964 Olympic Track and Field trials in Los Angeles, Cliff got out strong in the 400-meter hurdles and was on his way to making another Olympic team. However, when he stumbled over a hurdle, he was out of the race and his Olympic dream was over.

After that experience, Cliff wrote a letter to the newspaper in his hometown of Grand Forks, North Dakota, in which he encouraged young people not to feel sorry for him, but instead to set goals for themselves. His letter, written on an airplane only hours after the unfortunate fall, has been an inspiration to many.

After graduating from the University of Kansas in 1961, Cliff became a fighter pilot in the Air Force. In 1966, at the age of 28, as an athlete in the prime of his career, he was listed as missing in action in Vietnam. He left a wife and 10-month-old son. In 1975, Clifton E. Cushman was officially declared dead. But his timeless inspirational message lives on, daring people to become great.

Questions for Thought:

1. Cliff Cushman could have felt sorry for himself after seeing his Olympic gold medal dream shattered when he tripped over a hurdle. How did he respond?

2. What stands out to you in the, "I dare you letter?"

3. What are you willing to "dare to do" in order to become a better athlete?

I Dare You – Open Letter to Youth

"Don't feel sorry for me. I feel sorry for some of you! ... you watched me hit the fifth hurdle, fall and lie on the track in an inglorious heap of skinned elbows, bruised hips, torn knees, and injured pride, unsuccessful in my attempt to make the Olympic team a second time. In a split second all the many years of training, pain, sweat, blisters, and agony of running were simply and irrevocably wiped out. But I tried! I would much rather fall knowing I had put forth an honest effort than never to have tried at all.

"This is not to say everyone is capable of making the Olympic team. However, each of you is capable of trying to make your own 'Olympic team,' whether it be the high school football team, the glee club, the honor roll or whatever your goal may be. Unless your reach exceeds your grasp, how can you be sure what you can attain? And don't you think there are things better than cigarettes, hot rod cars, school dropouts, excessive makeup, and ducktail grease-cuts?

"Over 15 years ago I saw a star — first place in the Olympic Games. I literally started to run after it. In 1960, I came within three yards of grabbing it; this year I stumbled, fell and watched it recede four more years away. Certainly, I was very disappointed in falling flat on my face. However, there is nothing I can do about it now but get up, pick the cinders from my wounds, and take one step followed by one more, until the steps turn into the miles and miles of success.

"I know I may never make it. The odds are against me, but I have something in my favor — desire and faith. Romans 5:3-5 has always had an inspirational meaning to me ... 'we rejoice in our suffering, knowing that suffering produces endurance, and endurance produces character, and character produces hope, and hope does not disappoint us.'

"At least I am going to try. How about you? Would a little extra effort on your part bring up your grade average? Would you have a better chance to make the football team if you stayed an extra 15 minutes and worked on your blocking?

"Let me tell you something about yourselves. You are taller and heavier than any past generation in this country. You are spending more money, enjoying more freedom, and driving more cars ... yet many of you have never known the satisfaction of doing your best in sports, excelling in class, the wonderful feeling of completing a job, any job, and looking back on it knowing you have done your best.

"I dare you to have your hair cut and not wilt under the comments of your so-called friends. I dare you to clean up your language, I dare you to honor your mother and father. I dare you to go to church without being compelled by your parents. I dare you to unselfishly help someone less fortunate than you and enjoy the wonderful feeling that goes with it. I dare you to be physically fit. I dare you to read a book not required in school. I dare you to look up at the stars, not down in the mud, and set your sights on one of them that, up to now, you thought was unattainable. There is plenty of room at the top but no room for anyone to sit down.

"You may be surprised at what you can achieve with sincere effort. So get up, pick the cinders out of your wounds, and take one more step.

"I dare you!

Willie Davenport

Summer and Winter Olympian

Willie Davenport was born in Troy, Alabama, and began running the hurdles at Howland High School in Warren, Ohio. After high school, Willie became an Army paratrooper and a member of its track team. While serving in the military, he was the surprise winner in the 110-meter hurdles at the 1964 Olympic Trials, as he upset five-time national AAU champion Hayes Jones in the 110-meter high hurdles. Suddenly, he was the favorite to win a gold medal at the Olympics. Unfortunately, he pulled a thigh muscle two days before Olympic competition began and was unable to make the finals. The American athletes he had defeated in the Olympic Trials placed first and second. Willie continued to train and won the national championship for the next three consecutive years. After being discharged from the Army, he competed for Southern University in Louisiana.

His greatest moment came at the 1968 Mexico City Olympics, when he won the gold medal in the 110-meter hurdles with an Olympic record time of 13.3. Willie set a world record in 1969, but by 1972 there were new, young U.S. stars in the hurdles and Willie finished fourth at the Munich Olympics behind U.S. winner Rodney Milburn.

In 1975, Willie suffered a ruptured tendon in the national AAU meet in Eugene, Oregon. After the operation, a blood clot was found in his right knee and Willie spent much of the summer in the hospital. However, he overcame the injury to make his fourth Olympic team. At 33 years of age, Willie captured the Olympic bronze medal, less than one-tenth of a second behind the winner.

But Willie's Olympic days weren't over. The United States didn't participate in the 1980 Summer Olympics because of President Jimmy Carter's boycott, so Willie qualified and competed as part of the U.S. team in the four-man bobsled event at the Winter Olympics. He achieved a unique distinction in 1980 by becoming one of the few athletes to ever compete in both Summer and Winter Olympic Games. Willie and fellow bobsledder Jeff Gadley were the first black Olympic bobsledders, inspired by the myth that blacks couldn't compete in Winter Olympic sports.

Questions for Thought:

1. Willie showed his desire by making five Olympic teams. How do you channel your desire into success?

2. Willie was serving in the military and made the Olympic team. He was able to focus on one thing at a time to be successful. How do you focus on the task at hand and avoid outside distractions?

3. Willie overcame the myth that blacks were not good enough to compete in the Winter Olympics. Are there any myths that you have overcome? Think of other myths that great athletes have proven wrong.

Harrison Dillard

Good Things Come To Those Who Wait

Harrison Dillard began hurdling at the age of 8, setting up springs from abandoned car seats as barriers and jumping over them in an alley. In high school, Harrison was very successful, becoming a city and state champion. He attended college at Baldwin Wallace University, but his college years were interrupted when Dillard was called to active duty by the U.S. Army and served two and a half years.

After the war, Harrison went back to Baldwin Wallace to continue his education and was highly successful in track and field, winning numerous titles including National Collegiate Championships in 1946 and 1947 and setting world records in the 120-yard and 220-yard hurdles.

Because of the war, the Olympic Games of 1940 and 1944 were canceled. The revival of the Olympic Games was scheduled for England in 1948. Harrison entered the U.S. 1948 Olympic Trials in the 110-meter hurdles as the Olympic favorite. Harrison almost never hit hurdles when he ran, but that day, he hit the first hurdle and continued to hit hurdles, and suddenly the greatest hurdler in the world was out of the race. His Olympic dream of gold in the hurdles was shattered. Fortunately, he also ran the 100 meters, finishing behind fellow Americans Barney Ewell and Mel Patton, qualifying for the Olympic Games.

A capacity crowd of 75,000 people watched the Olympic Games 100-meter final. Harrison was a big underdog, but got out fast and held the lead the entire way to win Olympic gold. He also came back to add another gold as a member of the 4x100-meter relay team.

Harrison's career was astonishing. He held world records for the 120-yard and 110-meter hurdles, as well as the 220-yard and 200-meter hurdles. His record in the hurdles and sprints was 201 races won and only six lost. But yet, a spark still burned inside of him as he ached over his failure to win an Olympic medal in the hurdles. The 1952 Olympic Games were held in Helsinki, Finland, and Harrison qualified for the Olympic final in the 110-meter hurdles. Harrison led over the third hurdle, but Jack Davis closed fast. Harrison concentrated on maintaining full speed and was careful not to hit a hurdle. At the ninth hurdle, they were even and Harrison relied on his experience to drive over the 10th hurdle and sprint to the finish to win the race.

Harrison Dillard had waited through two Olympiads cancelled because of war, through an Olympiad where he had won gold, but not in his best event, to finally capture the race on which he had set his heart.

Questions for Thought:

1. Harrison had to wait 12 years to finally capture gold in the event he loved. Think of a time when you showed patience and it paid off.

2. How do you motivate yourself to stay committed over a long period of time to reach your goals?

3. Do you have a spark inside you that could lead to success? How do you ignite it?

Buddy Edelen

U.S. Distance Pioneer

In the early 1960s, distance running was not popular in the United States, as the running boom would not be ignited until a decade later. There was no money at road races and no sponsorship by shoe or apparel companies. Therefore, the name Leonard "Buddy" Edelen is not a household name. However, Buddy's success as a marathon runner inspired a generation of runners, including Olympic marathon champion Frank Shorter. As a high school senior, Buddy set records in every cross country and mile race he ran, culminating in a state mile record of 4:28.8. At Minnesota, he was the Big Ten cross country champion and the two mile track champion. However, Buddy enjoyed running longer distances and wanted to move up to the marathon. He realized that U.S. distance runners were not highly regarded by European athletes, and he was determined to change that.

He moved to England so he could train and race with the best marathon runners in the world. In 1962, he set an American record time of 2:18:57, making him the first American to run under 2:20:00 for the marathon. He was also the first American to run under 30 minutes for the 10,000-meter run. Between 1962 and 1967, Buddy won seven of the 13 marathons he ran against the best competition in the world, including the London marathon in a new world record of 2:14.28, becoming the first man to run under 2:15 for the distance.

Buddy taught school in England but returned to the U.S. for the 1964 Olympic Marathon Trials in Yonkers, New York. The race would be his greatest effort. It was run in brutal heat and humidity with temperatures between 90 and 100 degrees. A phenomenal 70 percent of the runners had to drop out because of the oppressive conditions. Buddy was feeling the effects of the heat, but his determination caused him to press on. Leading by a large, increasing margin as the race progressed, he kept pushing the pace, winning by 20 minutes in 2:24.25. However, he paid the price for his effort as he developed sciatic problems and finished a disappointing sixth place in the 1964 Olympic Games in Tokyo, Japan, behind champion Abebe Bikila of Ethiopia.

Buddy stopped competing at age 28 and became a professor at Adams State in Colorado, but forever remains a pioneer in U.S. distance running.

Questions for Thought:

1. Buddy Edelen wanted to run with the best, so he moved to where the competition was. Do you enjoy competing against great competition? How can good competition make you better?

2. Despite having a large lead in the Olympic Marathon Trials and suffering because of the heat, Buddy refused to back off and cruise in. What does it mean to run hard, but also run smart?

3. Buddy was a pioneer that helped set the stage for future runners such as gold medal marathoner Frank Shorter. How will you set the stage for athletes to come after you?

Hicham El Guerrouj

King of the Mile

Hicham El Guerrouj of Morroco competed in his first Olympic Games in 1996 in Atlanta at the age of 22. Hicham was expected to challenge the world record holder and three-time world champion, Noureddine Morceli, for the gold medal in the 1500 meters. The Olympic 1500-meter final was entering the final lap when El Guerrouj moved up along the outside of the front pack to challenge for the lead. Suddenly, he was tripped and fell hard to the track. By the time he could get up and start running again, he was several meters behind, was unable to move up and finished in last place.

El Guerrouj immediately set his sights on the 2000 Olympic Games, to be held in Sydney, Australia. In the years leading up to the 2000 Olympics, Hicham established himself as the best middle distance runner in the world, winning two world championship titles and setting both the 1500-meter and mile world records indoors and outdoors. He lowered the world record time in the mile to 3:43.13.

Hicham entered the 2000 Olympic Games as the overwhelming favorite. However, he ran a poor tactical race and he was only able to finish second in the 1500 meters behind Noah Ngeny, a Kenyan runner who had finished second in Hicham's 1500-meter world record race. Extremely disappointed, Hicham broke down in tears on the track.

Hicham continued his reign as the top 1500 meters and mile runner in the world, and he defended his 1500-meter title at the 2001 and 2003 World Championships. Despite being the best middle distance runner in the world, Hicham had not won an Olympic medal. His sights were set on gold in 2004 at the Athens, Greece Olympic Games. His 2004 season started off slowly and his times weren't where he wanted them to be. He even finished eighth in a 1500-meter race in Rome. Nonetheless, Hicham lined up for the 1500-meter final in Athens, determined to capture the gold that he had narrowly missed in two previous Olympics. Hicham fulfilled his dream as he won by a tenth of a second to win gold. A few days later, he out sprinted world record holder Kenenisa Bekele of Ethiopia in the final few meters of the 5000 meters to win a second gold. He became the first man in 80 years to win both 1500 meters and 5000-meter races in the same Olympics, a feat last achieved by the "Flying Finn," Paavo Nurmi, in 1924. Having accomplished his dream that he had dedicated his life to, Hicham El Geurrouj never again competed internationally.

Questions for Thought:

1. Twice misfortune struck, but Hicham never gave up. How do you handle misfortune? How quickly do you bounce back?

2. Hicham was willing to wait and worked eight years to achieve his goal. How much time do you put towards your goal? How much are you willing to put in?

3. Hicham won two gold medals in his last Olympics. Do you believe in the saying, "the greater the challenge the greater the reward?"

Herb Elliott

Undefeated

Herb Elliott stared running at the age of 8 and showed early promise as a schoolboy champion in Perth, Australia. However, in 1955, he injured his foot while moving a piano and gave up running.

In 1956, Herb travelled from Perth with his family to watch the Melbourne Olympics. Inspired by the best runners in the world, it awakened a new level of commitment in Herb. He did not return to Perth with his parents after the Olympics. He stayed to be coached by Percy Cerutty, an eccentric visionary who not only worked to improve the bodies of the athletes he coached, but also their minds. He challenged Herb not to beat opponents, but to conquer himself. Herb responded to the training of the body and the mind and began to dominate middle distance running.

Herb set the world record for the mile in 1958, running 3:54.5, and later that same season set the 1500-meter world record in 3:36.0. However, the two years of competitive running exhausted him and he drifted away from serious training. He got married and began studying at Cambridge University. But, as the 1960 Rome Olympics approached, he caught the competitive fire again and began training seriously. Six months before the Olympics, he joined up with his old coach, Percy Cerutty and began a rigorous training program, which included running in sand dunes. In the Olympic 1500-meter final, Elliott took the lead with 600 meters remaining, and stormed to a new world record time of 3:35.6.

The talented athlete retired at the age of 22, unbeaten in the 1500 meters and mile in 42 races from 1957 to 1961. Herb returned to the Olympics in the 2000 Sydney Games as one of the final bearers of the Olympic flame.

Questions for Thought:

1. Herb was undefeated in his career. What type of competitor do you have to be to win?

2. Watching great runners motivated Herb to resume training. Does watching great athletes perform motivate you?

3. Herb worked with Coach Cerutty on a rigorous training program. How do you work with others, such as coaches, to get improve? Do coaches push you further than you could push yourself?

Raymond Ewry

Legs of Steel

Public domain photo

You could say Raymond Ewry had a difficult childhood. He was born in Lafayette, Indiana, and became an orphan at the age of 5. At the age of 7, a doctor told Ray he had polio, which there was no cure for, and he would be bound to a wheelchair, never to walk again. One doctor suggested leg exercises as a last resort. Ray dreamed of getting out of the wheelchair, taking just one step, and being able to walk. Ray would do his exercises several hours a day. He would push himself out of his wheelchair and onto the ground, and teach himself to stand. After he could balance himself on his two feet, he began to jump. The crippled boy eventually developed legs of steel.

Ray enrolled at University of Purdue and broke world records in the standing high jump, standing long jump, and standing triple jump. After college, he joined the New York Athletic Club, whose members had taken a strong interest in the inaugural Olympic Games in 1896 in Athens. In 1900, the Olympics were to be held for the second time in Paris, with the New York Athletic Club and Ray competing.

The early Olympic Games consisted of several events such as the standing long, standing triple jump, and standing high jump. These events are no longer contested in current Olympic Games. In the standing high jump, competitors took one step and jumped. Ray jumped 5-5 to win. In the standing long jump, Ray leapt 10-10 to win. In the standing triple jump, Ray covered 34-8½. The French gave Ray the nickname, "The Human Frog."

In the 1904 Olympics in St. Louis, Ray won the same three events again. Two years later, Athens, Greece, was celebrating the 10th anniversary of the modern Games with an extra Olympics competition. Although 1906 was not an Olympic year, the medals counted and Ray won two more. The boy with polio had become the unbeatable Olympic champion. Ray won two more gold medals in London in the 1908 Olympics and retired with 10 gold medals. No other Olympian in history has won as many gold medals without losing a single Olympic competition.

Raymond Ewry, the child who wasn't supposed to take a single step, became one of the greatest jumpers in Olympic history.

Questions for Thought:

1. How has your childhood affected your career?

2. Ray Ewry worked for hours with little progress to show until eventually he developed legs of steel. How long are you willing to work to achieve a goal?

3. Ray was a winner. How would you define being a winner?

Dick Fosbury
The Flop

Dick Fosbury began his high jump career using the scissors jumping style. His high school coach encouraged him to use the straddle jump, which was the popular style of jumping at the time. But Dick struggled to use the straddle technique and went back to using the scissors, which he modified by going over the bar backward. His "flop" technique involved going over the bar headfirst and backward, with his body horizontal to the ground. In previous years, sawdust, sand, or wood chip surfaces had been used as the landing pit and jumpers using the scissors, roll or straddle techniques were able to clear the bar while upright and then land on their feet. Dick's style required him to land on his back, and fortunately high schools and colleges were starting to replace its sawdust, sand, or wood chip landing pits with foam rubber pits, enabling high jumpers to land more safely. The new technique quickly became known as "the Fosbury flop" and revolutionized the high jump.

Dicks's new technique worked so well that he improved by an entire foot in high school, from 5-3¾ to 6-3¾. Dick went to college at Oregon State University and first cleared 7-0 during the 1968 indoor season. He won two NCAA high jump championships and qualified for the U.S. Olympic team.

At the 1968 Mexico City Olympics, Dick cleared 7-4¼ on his third and final attempt to become the surprise winner and set the Olympic and American records. Four years later, in the 1972 Olympic Games, 70 percent of the high jumpers used the "Fosbury flop" technique and it evolved into the most commonly used high jumping technique in the world.

Questions for Thought:

1. Dick Fosbury's lack of success at jumping caused him to create a new technique that led to great success. Have you ever changed something that led to greater success?

2. People laughed at Dick when they first saw his style. Are you afraid to try new things because you think people will laugh at you or you will fail?

3. Dick's new style coincided with the use of a safer landing pit. How does good equipment help you to perform?

Robert Garrett

Novice Olympic Champion

When Robert Garrett arrived at the 1896 Olympics, he had never touched a real discus. The discus was not part of U.S. track and field in those days. He had seen a discus painted on an ancient vase a few months earlier, so he had a blacksmith make a homemade disc. An official discus weighs less than 5 pounds, but Garrett's discus was over 25 pounds heavier and 4 inches wider. He could barely lift it, let alone throw it, so he gave up on the idea of throwing it in the Olympics.

When he arrived at the Olympics in Athens, Greece, Robert was surprised to see a regulation discus. He took a couple of practice throws and decided to enter the competition. The Greeks prided themselves on the discus and emphasized style. However, the inexperienced Garrett's first two throws were awkward and clumsy, almost hitting spectators. Everyone, including Robert, laughed at his throws. His third and final throw however sailed to a mark of 95-6 and amazingly won the Olympic competition. The Greeks were stunned over having been defeated at their own event. Robert Garrett had won the Olympic title without a single day of practice with the implement!

The first American Olympians in 1896 were surprisingly successful at the first Olympic Games, winning 11 Olympic championships and starting the U.S. Olympic movement. The American team left for the 1896 Olympics in Athens with little support from U.S. officials or the public. Thrown together at the last minute and a collection of collegians paying their own way, they achieved a level of excellence that stunned everyone and became overnight sensations. Had they not succeeded, it's very likely the American Olympic movement would have died or have been delayed for years.

Robert also won the Olympic shot put with a throw of 36-8 and finished second in the high jump and second in the long jump. After his 1896 success, he returned to place third in the shot put and the standing triple jump in the 1900 Olympics. He also competed in the discus but due to a unique discus area, all of his throws hit trees within the throwing sector.

Questions for Thought:

1. Robert Garrettt quickly adapted once he picked up a regulation discus. How important is being able to adapt to the situation?

2. What are some ways that you could become more adaptable?

3. The first U.S. Olympians surprised many people with their success. How might surprising people with success contribute to motivation?

Johnny Gray

Taking Out The Pace

Photo Courtesy of USATF

Johnny Gray became the greatest 800-meter runner in U.S. history by bravely taking the pace out hard to set up fast runs. Johnny originally went out for track at Crenshaw High in Los Angeles to run the two mile event. However, his high school coach thought he had better potential in the 800 meters. His senior year in high school he improved by 15 seconds and won the Los Angeles city title.

Johnny's brilliant career was one of longevity and quality. For 14 straight seasons, Johnny ran faster than 1:45 for 800 meters. He won the United States Olympic Track and Field Trials three times, made four Olympic teams and is considered to be one of the finest 800-meter runners in U.S. history. He set the U.S. outdoor 800 meters record on five occasions, with his fastest being a 1:42.60 in 1985. He won the U.S. outdoor 800-meter championships seven times and was ranked in the top ten in the world for 11 years and ranked No. 1 in the U.S. eight times by "Track & Field News."

Johnny Gray's racing tactics can be best described as gutsy. He was not afraid to step out of his comfort zone and push the pace. He led the Olympic 800-meter race at the 1992 Summer Olympics with a blazing first lap at faster than world record pace. In going out fast in a race, the body responds physiologically by producing waste product, which accumulates and leads to muscle inhibition and fatigue later in the race. Despite his best efforts to go all out and give it everything he had, he began to fatigue in the latter stages of the race and was passed twice during the final lap to end up in third place. A reporter later asked him what he would have done differently if he could run the race a second time, and he responded, "I would have taken it out harder." Runners refer to such an attitude as "taking it to the Gray zone" in his honor.

Questions for Thought:

1. Johnny Gray ran through the pain to challenge himself and his competitors to run fast. Do you have the strength to try something that feels uncomfortable?

2. What are you willing to put on the line to be successful?

3. Have you taken it to the "Gray zone" before? How did it feel when you took it to that zone? How did it feel after you had recovered?

Murray Halberg

Courage Down Under

Murray Halberg exemplifies the Olympic spirit of overcoming adversity. As a rugby player in New Zealand in his youth, Murray suffered a severe injury during a game, leaving his left arm crippled. He had to teach himself to do everything, from writing to eating, with his right hand. From the injury arose the will and the courage of a champion. The next year, he took up running, determined to overcome his handicap.

In 1951, Murray met a man named Arthur Lydiard, who became his coach. Lydiard had been a famous long distance runner and he had new ideas on how to train of athletes. It took Murray a while to mature as an athlete under Lydiard. In the 1956 Olympic Games in Melbourne, Australia, he reached the final of the 1500 meters, but ran a poor tactical race, slipping back through the field to finish almost last. Devastated, he vowed to himself that he would return to the Olympic stage and fulfill his destiny of becoming an Olympic champion.

In 1958, he became the first New Zealander to break 4:00 in the mile, becoming the first great athlete to emerge from the Arthur Lydiard coached group. By 1960, he was favored to win the Olympic 5000-meter title. He and Lydiard decided on the bold tactic of sprinting with three laps remaining and then holding on.

Motivated by his training partner Peter Snell's victory in the 800-meter final just 20 minutes before his race, Murray carried out the race plan perfectly, putting 20 meters on the field with his sudden burst and holding on to win by 10 meters.

He ran again at the Tokyo Olympics in 1964 in the 10,000 meters and finished seventh. After he retired from running, he did some coaching, but eventually poured his time and energy into the Halberg Trust, which supports children with disabilities to be active in sport, creation, and leisure.

Questions for Thought:

1. Murray had to give up one sport, but it only motivated him to focus more on running. Have you ever had to give up something and were disappointed, but it motivated you to do better at something else?

2. Murray worked with Coach Lydiard to develop race plans and carry them out. How much courage does it take to carry out the race plan Murray had for the 1960 Olympics?

3. Murray won gold just 20 minutes after his training mate did. How do your teammates motivate you? How do you motivate your teammates?

Franklin Jacobs

Small Man- Big Leap

In 1979, Farleigh Dickson University's (FDU) Franklin Jacobs was a rising star in track and field. He was undefeated, ranked No. 1 in the world indoors, and had set a world high jump record of 7-8¼ at the prestigious Millrose Games. He was a favorite for a medal at the 1980 Olympics.

Franklin stood only 5-8 and didn't start high jumping until his senior year in high school when he cleared 6-8, winning the state championship. He had an amazing vertical leap of 44 inches and cleared a high jump bar an astounding 23 inches over his head.

On a January night in 1978, in New York City, the Millrose Games high jump had become a two-man duel between Jacobs and the defending champion, Olympian Dwight Stones. The event turned strategic as Stones, known for his gamesmanship, suggested to Franklin they put the bar at a world-record height. Stones, ahead on fewer misses in the competition, figured both would not clear the record height so early in the season and he would win the competition on fewer misses. Both jumpers missed on their first two attempts to clear 7-8¼ . Franklin moved his approach back to 14 steps for additional speed in the run-up and it worked. Stones' plan had backfired and Franklin had set a new world record with the crowd of 19,000 erupting with delight. In the process, he not only beat Stones but also the gold and silver medalists from the 1976 Montreal Olympics.

As quickly as Franklin appeared on the scene, he disappeared; his dreams dashed with the U.S. Olympic boycott of the 1980 Moscow Summer Games. The United States held the Olympic Trials in 1980 in Eugene, Oregon. Franklin decided to let the bar go to 7-3 before he started jumping. He planned to clear the height and stop in protest. Unfortunately, he missed all three attempts.

Questions for Thought:

1. Have you ever been talked out of doing something because people said you could not do it?

2. How does it feel to accomplish something when you beat the odds?

3. Through training, Franklin Jacobs was able to overcome his lack of height. If you have some physical limits, how will you overcome them?

Bruce Jenner

Hard Work to Reach a Goal

William Bruce Jenner was embarrassed that he had a reading disability that caused him to fail second grade, and he began to focus his energy on sports. He credited his learning disability for giving him his intense drive to succeed. Because nothing came easy to him, he had to work harder, and he realized the way to get ahead in life is through hard work.

While in high school, he was a pole vault and high jump state champion, and he played basketball and football as well. He went to Graceland College in Lamoni, Iowa, on a $250 per year football scholarship. However, his freshman year, he was sidelined by a football injury and became bored, so he turned to the decathlon. Bruce was immediately successful. He won his first meet, setting a school record of 6,991 points. He decided to devote all his energy to the decathlon.

Bruce went to the 1972 U.S. Olympic Trials but was not expected to finish in the top three and make the team. On the second day, with three events left, he was in 10th place. After the pole vault, he moved to seventh place and after the javelin, into fifth place. To make the Olympic team, he had to beat the third place athlete by 18 seconds in the final event, the 1500 meters. Bruce beat him by 21 seconds to make the U.S. team. He traveled to Munich, Germany, to compete in the 1972 Olympic Games and finished in 10th place. He was disappointed in his finish, and vowed to train harder.

Bruce trained eight hours a day to prepare for the next Olympic Games. He even put hurdles in his living room and trained over them. His rigorous training regime paid dividends, as he made dramatic improvement. He moved up in the rankings and by the time the 1976 Olympic Games in Montreal arrived, Bruce was one of the favorites.

By the end of the first day, he was only 35 points behind the leader and was confident in his abilities as a strong competitor on the second day. By the eighth event, he had taken control of the decathlon and went on to win, setting a new world record with 8,176 points. After thousands of hours of training and committing to a goal, Bruce Jenner had reached his goal and retired after the 1976 Olympics.

Bruce used his Olympic fame to develop a career as an entrepreneur, product spokesperson, and motivational speaker. Bruce's face appeared on the Wheaties box as an example of athletic prowess and health, and he went on to work and star in the television and film industry.

Questions for Thought:

1. Bruce was motivated by his learning disability. Is there anything you struggle with that motivates you to work harder?

2. When Bruce Jenner finished 10th in his first Olympics, he was motivated to improve. Have you had success at a task, but knew you could do even better if you continued to work on it?

3. On a scale of 1-10 (10 high) how would you rate your commitment to your work?

Michael Johnson

Double World Records

Photo Courtesy of USATF

In Michael Johnson's great career, he won four Olympic gold medals and set world records at 200 meters, 400 meters, and the 4x400-meter relay. He had an outstanding high school career as a sprinter at Skyline High School in Dallas, Texas. In Michael's freshman year at Baylor University, he broke the Baylor school record at 200 meters, running 20.41 in his first collegiate meet. However, a pulled hamstring cost him a majority of the season.

Michael continued to improve his sophomore year at Baylor, and was ranked seventh in the United States, but was disqualified from a 200-meter heat at the NCAA indoor meet. As he trained for the Olympic Trials, further bad luck struck as he developed a stress fracture in his left fibula and was unable to make the Olympic team. By the time of his graduation from Baylor, he had won five NCAA Championships and became the first athlete to be ranked No. 1 in the world in both the 200 meters and 400 meters.

After graduation, Michael shifted his focus to winning the 200 meters at the 1992 Olympics. Michael continued to train in Waco, Texas, with coach Clyde Hart, who was considered one of the best 400-meter coaches in the world. Right before the Barcelona Olympics, Michael developed food poisoning. With his energy levels extremely low, he failed to run fast enough to qualify for the 200-meter final. He was able to come back and win a gold medal on the winning United States 4x400-meter relay team, but he knew it wasn't the same as an individual gold.

The 1996 Atlanta Olympics was Michael's time to shine. At the Olympic Trials he showed he was ready by running 19.66 in the 200 meters to break Pietro Mennea's world record of 19.72, which had stood for 17 years. He also won the 400 meters to set up an unprecedented attempt to win both the 200 meters and 400 meters at the Olympics. On July 29, 1996, Michael Johnson started his record-breaking streak by winning the 400-meter dash in 43.49, a new Olympic record. Three days later he shattered the 200 meters world record in 19.32, the largest improvement ever on a 200-meter world record. Experts have compared that performance to the great long jump by Bob Beamon in the 1968 Olympic Games.

Questions for Thought:

1. Michael Johnson was the best 200-meter runner in the world but couldn't prove it because of food poisoning. Do you think you are really good at something? How do you prove it?

2. Michael challenged himself with a very tough 200 and 400-meter double. Do you take on challenges to make yourself better? How does your body and mind respond to the challenge?

3. Michael had a good support system in coach Hart. How do you use your support system to help reach your goals?

Rafer Johnson

Role Model

Rafer Johnson was raised in an atmosphere of segregation, discrimination, and poverty in Texas. The Johnson family lived in poverty and at one time even lived in a railroad boxcar for a year. Rafer's athletic career nearly ended before it began when, as a young boy, his left foot was severely cut when it was caught in a conveyor belt.

In high school, Rafer was a superb all-around athlete, winning varsity letters in football, baseball, basketball, and track. In baseball, he hit above .400. In basketball, he averaged 17 points a game, and in football he led the team to three league championships, averaging nine yards a carry as a running back. However, his best sport was track and field.

At UCLA, he turned to the decathlon and in only his fourth decathlon, he broke the world record. He qualified for both the decathlon and the long jump in the 1956 Summer Olympic Games in Melbourne, Australia. However, Rafer suffered an injury before the competition and had to forfeit his place in the long jump. Still suffering from the injury, he finished second behind fellow American Milton Campbell in the decathlon. That would be the last defeat for Rafer in the decathlon.

A car accident one year before the 1960 Rome Olympics left Rafer Johnson with a severely injured back. He spent several weeks in the hospital but recovered enough to win the Olympic Trials. Rafer's biggest challenge in winning the Olympic decathlon was his training partner and fellow UCLA decathlete C.K. Yang of Taiwan. Both trained under legendary UCLA track coach Elvin C. "Ducky" Drake and become close friends. After the first nine events, Johnson led Yang, but Yang was thought to be capable of overcoming this gap in the final event, the 1500 meters. Johnson, however, managed to cling on to Yang in the last event and won the gold. Rafer compiled an Olympic record 8,392 points and earned the title of the greatest all-round athlete in the world. At the age of 25, he had fulfilled his dream of being an Olympic decathlon champion.

Rafer Johnson had the unique ability to overcome both childhood poverty and a severe injury to fulfill his dream of becoming an Olympic champion. He has given his time to serve others, especially in representing the Special Olympics and promoting recreational activities for youth.

Questions for Thought:

1. Rafer overcame a challenging period as a youth to turn into an exemplary role model. Who are you a role model to?

2. Knowing that you are a role model to someone, how does that affect your actions?

3. Rafer's teammate, C.K. Yang, challenged him in practice every day and challenged him to win the gold medal. How does having other talented people around every day help you?

Al Joyner

Dream Chaser

Al Joyner grew up in East St. Louis, Illinois. His father was not around, but he was influenced by the strong guidance of his mother. She kept Al off the streets, urged him to get jobs, encouraged him, and taught him to be a man. In 1981, while Al was attending Arkansas State University, his mother suffered a massive hemorrhage and was in a coma with no brain activity. Al rushed home, and with his sister, Jackie, had to make a difficult decision to turn off the respirator that kept his mother alive. He vowed that he would honor his mother by winning the gold medal in the triple jump at the 1984 Olympics.

At Arkansas State University, Al became a six-time NCAA All-American. He continued to improve and in 1983, placed eighth in the world championships triple jump. He made sacrifices in his training, such as moving to Los Angeles to work out with UCLA coach Bob Kersee.

He qualified for the 1984 Olympic Games and was expected to be the third American behind Michael Conley and Willie Banks. In the qualifying jumps of the Olympics, he tweaked an ankle on his first jump and fouled on his second. His entire Olympics came down to a final all-or-nothing jump. He thought of his mother, focused on his breathing, and jumped 55-9½ to make the final. The next day for the final he was in the zone, jumping a lifetime best 56-7½ on his first jump. He took the lead and the pressure was on everyone else.

As Al was competing, he cheered on his sister Jackie, who went on to win silver in the heptathlon. In one of the biggest upsets of the 1984 Olympic Games, Al won the gold medal in the triple jump. He became the first American in 80 years to win a gold medal in the triple jump and received the 1984 Jim Thorpe Award given annually to the top American male in the field events.

Questions for Thought:

1. Al Joyner dreamed he would win the Olympics to honor his mother. What goes into making a dream become a reality?

2. Al's mother steered Al down the right path. Who has been an important mentor in your life?

3. Have you told those who have influenced your life that you appreciate them?

Alberto Juantorena

Stamina and Speed of a Horse

Alberto Juantorena's first love while growing up in Cuba was basketball until a track coach discovered his talent and convinced him to start running. Within a few months he rapidly improved and ran 48.2 for 400 meters. Only a year later, Alberto was running in the 1972 Munich Olympic Games, but was eliminated in the semifinals of the 400 meters.

Over the next two years, Alberto was unbeaten in the 400 meters. He overcame two foot operations to emerge as the favorite in the 400 meters for the 1976 Olympics. He earned the nickname "El caballo" (the horse) because of his powerful three meter long strides.

In 1976, his coach persuaded him to try racing at 800 meters. Alberto was primarily a sprinter, and many experts felt he was far too muscular at 6-2 and 185 pounds to compete with the thin runners in the distance events. He surprised people when he clocked 1:44.9, the second-fastest 800 meters of the year. Alberto decided to attempt the unusual double of the 400 meters and 800 meters at the Montreal Olympic Games, despite the fact he had only run the 800 meters four times, and all of them were during the Olympic year of 1976.

Running the 400 meters in the Olympics involves running preliminary rounds. Alberto had to run several qualifying races to make the final. Alberto had to have considerable stamina to make it through all the qualifying rounds. Few thought "El Caballo" would be capable of running the 400 meter qualifying rounds and still be able to maintain his stamina through three rounds of Olympic-caliber 800 meters.

In the 800-meter final in Montreal, Alberto quickly established the lead, running the first 400 meters in 50.85. At 600 meters, Alberto was briefly challenged, but then powered away from his opposition, winning the gold medal easily in a new world record time of 1:43.50.

Three days later, he attempted to win the 400 meters and took the lead in the last 20 meters to win his second gold medal, becoming the only runner in Olympic history to achieve a 400 and 800 meters double victory.

Questions for Thought:

1. Alberto Juantorena stepped out of his comfort zone for the 400-800 challenge. Think of a time you stepped out of your comfort zone. What made you get out of your zone?

2. What obstacles are in the way of you getting out of your comfort zone?

3. How can you overcome obstacles and step up to the challenge of competing out of your comfort zone?

Kip Keino

Roho: Honor and Courage

One of the greatest middle-distance races in history took place at the 1968 Olympic Games with world record holder Jim Ryun of Wichita, Kansas, and Kenyan Kip Keino. Kip would try an unprecedented Olympic triple: the 1500, 5000, and 10,000 meters. Kip ran the 10,000 meters first, and he ran with the leaders through the first 22 of the race's 25 laps. Suddenly, he collapsed onto the infield, stricken with abdominal pain that had bothered him all summer. Doctors diagnosed it as a gallbladder infection and advised him not to continue to run. Yet two days later, he was racing in the 5000 meters, qualifying for the final. Two days later, he claimed the silver medal at 5000 meters. In the 1500 meters, he ran the prelims, semifinals, and qualified for the final.

The Olympic 1500 final was held on October 28, 1968. Ryun entered as the favorite, Kip was running his sixth race of the week. Kip went out fast with a deliberate strategy to take away the devastating kick of world record holder Jim Ryun. Kip passed the 800-meter mark in 1:55.3, a world record pace considered impossible to sustain at altitude. The field expected Kip to come back to them, but as he entered the third lap and fatigue began to set in, "roho" became a factor. It's a Swahili word that means "heart and courage." In a competitive sense, "roho" means the capacity to strive beyond normal limits, to summon extraordinary effort in a crisis. As Kip recalled, "This is the race of my life, if I am going to die, let me die here." On the final lap, Ryun was flying, passing runners to move into second, but to everyone's surprise, he wasn't gaining on Kip. Kip drove hard off the final turn, his teeth bared in ferocious concentration, utterly focused on what he had resolved to do on the track. He hit the tape in 3:34.9, an Olympic record and the second fastest 1500-meter run in history. Ryun was a distant second in 3:37.8.

Kip was ready to suffer, to set a pace so fast that Ryun couldn't stay with it, and then hold on. Even though his chest was exploding and his legs turned to lead, Kip Keino had the ability to push beyond ordinary limits. His "roho" produced one of the most stunning performances ever.

Questions for Thought:

1. What does "roho" mean?

2. Why do you believe Kip Keino was successful?

3. How can you use the concept of "roho" to become a better athlete?

John Kuck

Champp With The Broken Ankle

Photo Courtesy of Emporia State University Athletics

John Henry Kuck was an Olympic champion who set more than 100 records in the shot put, javelin, and discus during his remarkable career. Born in Wilson, Kansas, he set national high school records in three events: the javelin, discus, and shot put in 1924 for Wilson High School.

After high school, John attended Kansas State Teachers College, now Emporia State University, where he was the 1926 national collegiate champion and a world record holder in both the shot put and the javelin. After his sophomore year, John dropped out of college and competed for the Kansas City Athletic Club and then the Olympic Club out of San Francisco. He was one of the first to record distances of over 50 feet with the 16-pound shot put, 210 feet with the javelin, and 140 feet with the discus.

He entered the 1928 Olympic Games in Amsterdam as one of the top three contenders in the shot put. The world record holder was Emil Hischfeld of Germany. A second American, Herman Brix, who would later go on to play Tarzan in Hollywood, was also a contender. On his first throw, Brix set a new Olympic record in the first round of the qualification with a 51-8¾ throw. Hischfeld threw 51-7 on his first throw and John, with a throw of 50-7½ on his third throw, could only move into third place.

The best six shot putters qualified for the final, where they attempted three more throws. Brix led the competition, followed by Hischfeld in second, and then John Kuck. The places remained unchanged through the first throw of the final until John stepped in the ring and exploded with a new world record of 52-0¾, breaking the previous world record by almost 13 inches.

Never before in Olympic competition had had anyone thrown 51-0, and no one had ever thrown more than 52 feet. On the afternoon of July 29, 1928, the three giants—two Americans and one German—were making history. In the final round of throws, the athletes were unable to improve on their marks, and John Kuck was the Olympic Champion.

What made John Kuck's Olympic victory and Olympic record even more impressive? He was nursing a broken left ankle at the Olympics.

Questions for Thought:

1. The 1928 Olympics brought the best out of John Kuck. How do you respond to great competition?

2. John was nursing a broken ankle but was able to come from behind to win. What do you focus on when you are behind?

3. John held records in the shot, discus, and javelin. How do you plan and organize to be able to multi-task?

Michael Larrabee

Persistence Pays

At the age of 30, Michael Larrabee became the oldest man to win the Olympic 400-meter title. Michael was a high school math teacher with an injury-plagued track career when he decided to make a run at the 1964 Olympic Games in Tokyo. His students laughed when he told them of his plan and the principal advised him that he "needed to face reality" at his age, which was considered ancient for a sprinter. However, Michael didn't give up on his dream.

After emerging as a young talent in the mid-1950s, Michael overcame several serious injuries; a severely strained hamstring and a ruptured right Achilles' tendon that caused him to miss out on the 1956 and 1960 Olympics. After those injuries healed, he faced another setback during the 1964 season because of an inflamed pancreas, the result of a blow by one of his high school students during a playful karate fight.

At the United States Olympic Trials in Los Angeles on September 12, 1964, Michael powered away from the field to tie the 400-meter world record of 44.9. Five weeks later on October 19, the final of the 1964 Olympic Games in Tokyo was run in wet conditions. Michael ran a very cautious first 300 meters and was in fifth place. He accelerated the final 100 meters, and with only 10 meters to go, he ran down Trinidad's Wendell Mottley to take the Olympic title in 45.1. Motley was a close second in 45.2. Michael Larrabee became the oldest man to win an Olympic 400 meters until 33-year-old Michael Johnson of the United States won the 400 at the 2000 Games in Sydney. Michael Larrabee was also a part of another world record when the USA team won the 4x400-meter relay gold in Tokyo in a time of 3:00.7.

Despite injuries that caused him to miss two Olympics, Michael Larrabee never gave up on his dreams. His persistence paid off with Olympic gold.

Questions for Thought:

1. How do you react when someone says you can't achieve something?

2. Think of a dream you have. How persistent are you in striving to reach your dream?

3. Do you give up easily when things don't go your way? Think of some ideas that would get you back on course.

Carl Lewis

King Carl

Carl Lewis was born into a track family. His father Bill ran track and his mother Evelyn was a world-class hurdler. As a youth Carl was small and skinny, and at first he lost many more competitions than he won. However, his dedication and commitment led to improvement and his senior year in high school, he was one of the top-ranked high school track athletes in the country.

Carl attended the University of Houston. After his freshman year he qualified for the 1980 Olympic team, but President Jimmy Carter cancelled U.S. participation. After winning NCAA Championships in both the 100 meters and the 200 meters, Carl turned professional, running with the Santa Monica Track Club. As the 1984 Olympic Games in Los Angeles approached, Carl announced he would win four gold medals. He backed up his talk winning the long jump, and the 4x100-meter relay, and the 100 and 200 meters in world record time. The four gold medals equaled the great Jesse Owens performance in the 1936 Olympics. Writers mocked Carl as "King Carl" for his brash predictions.

At the 1988 Olympic Games in Seoul, South Korea, Carl ran second to Ben Johnson, who won the 100-meter event in record time. However, Carl was awarded the gold medal soon afterward when Johnson was found to have illegally used steroids. Carl won his second gold medal in Seoul in the long jump. However, his success did little to improve his popularity in the United States. With a streak of 65 consecutive victories in the long jump, Carl had been the premier long jumper in the world for 10 years and had a goal of breaking Bob Beamon's long jump world record set at the 1968 Olympic Games. The stage was set for Carl to break the record at the 1991 World Championships. Carl set four personal records in the competition, but in the greatest long jump competition ever, it was American Mike Powell who broke the world record with a jump of 29-2½.

Carl failed to qualify for the 100-meters and 200-meters at the 1992 Olympic Trials, but qualified for the long jump and the 400-meter relay. Considered past his prime, Lewis responded like a champion when he beat Powell in the 1992 Olympic long jump to earn his third consecutive long jump gold medal. He anchored the 400-meter relay team to victory for his eighth overall career gold. Fans were beginning to admire the efforts of Carl Lewis. In his final Olympics in 1996 in Atlanta, Carl won his fourth straight gold medal in the long jump. After a brilliant career that saw him qualify for the U.S. Olympic team five times, he was finally accepted as a track and field legend.

Questions for Thought:

1. Although he won four gold medals in a single Olympics, Carl was considered brash and cocky. How should one act on and off the track for people to respect him or her?

2. There is a fine line between being cocky and confident. How can you be confident in your ability without being cocky?

3. After a long and successful career, Carl began to become popular with fans. Why?

Eric Liddell

Pure Gold

Public Domain Photo

Eric Liddell was born in China in 1902 to Scottish missionaries. He went to school in China until the age of 5, when he was enrolled in a boarding school in England. Eric participated in cricket and made the Scottish national rugby team as a youth before his natural running ability began to emerge.

The 1924 Olympics were in Paris, France. Eric had become one of the top sprinters in the world and was the favorite to win the 100 meters. When the Olympics' schedule was published months before the games, a 100-meter heat was scheduled for a Sunday. However, Eric was a devout Christian and refused to run in a heat held on the Sabbath. A man of strong principles, Eric withdrew from his best event, the 100 meters. Eric had limited previous success in the 400 meters, but since the 400-meter was not being held on a Sunday, he could participate in that event. He had also been selected to run as a member of the 4x100-meter and 4x400-meter relay teams at the Olympics, but declined to run those as their heats were to be run on a Sunday as well.

Eric first competed in the 200 meters and won the bronze medal in Paris. He went to the starting line of the 400-meter race as a big underdog. Before 1928, the 400 meters was considered a middle distance event in which runners raced the first curve and coasted through the backstretch. Eric ran hard the entire first 200 meters to get ahead of the favored Americans. The Americans challenged him all the way down the home straight, but Eric held on to take the win, breaking the Olympic record with a time of 47.6.

At the peak of his athletic career, Eric left Scotland to devote his life to being a missionary in China. Eric chose to live a dangerous life in China, serving his God. His greatness of heart and unwavering conviction are an inspiration to people of faith everywhere. In 1941, life in China had become dangerous because of Japanese aggressiveness. Despite suffering many hardships, Eric refused to leave. The Japanese imprisoned Eric, and suffering from overwork and malnourishment, he died of a brain tumor in a prison camp a few months before the end of World War II. Eric's story was portrayed in the popular movie, Chariots of Fire. Eric Liddell upheld the Olympic motto, "Citius, Altius, Fortius" which means, "Swifter, Higher, Stronger," throughout his life.

Questions for Thought:

1. Eric's beliefs were so strong that he was willing to give up Olympic glory. On a scale of 1-10 (10 high), how strong are your beliefs?

2. There is a saying, "if you don't stand for something, you will fall for anything." What do you stand for?

3. Eric had a passion to help people and gave his life for it. What sacrifices have you made to help people?

Gerry Lindgren

Young Phenom

Gerry Lindgren loved to run. During high school he ran twice a day, up to 110 to 120 miles a week. He knocked an astonishing 46 seconds off the high school two mile record to 8:40.0. Later that spring, he set a prep record (13:44.0) for 5000 meters. The 18-year-old stunned the track world with an inspiring 10,000-meter victory in the 1964 USA-USSR meet in Los Angeles. In the six-year history of the meet, the Americans had never won the 10,000. The two Soviets led early in the race, but Gerry ran close to them. Approaching the four-mile mark, he was barely hanging on when U.S coach Sam Bell called out for him to lead. The youthful Gerry Lindgren, fighting off fatigue, summoned up the courage to pass the veteran Soviet Union runners by sprinting for an entire lap to open up a 15-meter lead. In the back of his mind, Gerry questioned his own move. "Was it too early? Will I pay the price later?" The crowd, surprised to see him in the lead, cheered so loud that Gerry thought the Russians were gaining. Without letting up, Gerry crossed the finish line and turned to see the Russians 150 meters behind.

He went into the Tokyo Olympics as one of the favorites for the 10,000 meters. However, shortly before the Olympic 10,000-meter run in Tokyo, Gerry sprained an ankle. Valiantly, he ran in the 10,000-meter final and led at the 4,000-meter mark, but the ankle affected him and he slowed to finish in ninth place.

Gerry enrolled at Washington State in 1965 and won 11 NCAA championships in cross country and indoor and outdoor track, breaking the record of eight championships set by Jesse Owens at Ohio State. He was one of only two people to ever defeat Steve Prefontaine in an NCAA Championship. As he prepared for the 1968 Olympics, disaster struck in the form of a strained Achilles tendon. He finished fifth in the 10,000 meters and fourth in the 5000 meters at the trials, barely missing the team.

Gerry trained hard with the 1972 Olympics in Munich as the goal. He ran a staggering 50 miles a day during one training stretch. But two weeks before the Olympic Trials, he injured his knee when he had a collision with a car. Later that year, Gerry joined the pro track tour, the International Track Association, but the association folded in 1976. Although Olympic glory passed him by, Gerry Lindgren is still remembered as one of the greatest U.S. distance runners.

Questions for Thought:

1. Gerry Lindgren had trouble making the high school cross country team until he made a commitment to increase his mileage. What type of commitment are you willing to make?

2. Gerry was not afraid to take the lead in the race against the Russians, and had the courage to make a winning move. What does it take to show courage in the face of fatigue?

3. Gerry ran a staggering 50 miles a day for one training stretch. However, he also had a history of injuries, perhaps overuse injuries from overtraining. What does it mean to train hard, but train smart?

Lopez Lomong

The Lost Boy of Sudan

When Lopez Lomong was 6 years old, he was one of more than 100 young boys kidnapped by government soldiers from Sunday Catholic mass in his native country, Sudan. They were taken to a prison where they were trained as child soldiers. However, Lopez escaped with three friends though a narrow gap in the prison fence and ran for three days until they crossed the border into Kenya. They spent 10 years in a Kenyan refugee camp run by Catholic missionaries. At the refugee camp, Lopez had only one meal a day. He played soccer to forget about his hunger.

Lopez lived as a refugee for more than a decade, convinced he would spend his life at the camp. Despite being separated from his family, he considered himself lucky. Thousands of boys drowned, were eaten by wild animals, or were shot by military forces in Sudan. With the help of the Catholic Refugees Relief Operation, Lopez was among 3,800 Sudanese boys to arrive in the United States in a program that would be known as the "Lost Boys of Sudan."

Once in the U.S., Lopez became a naturalized citizen and started running. He won a New York state high school championship, and went on to college at Northern Arizona University. He was the NCAA indoor champion at 3000 meters, and the outdoor champion at 1500 meters.

One year after gaining his U.S. citizenship, Lopez qualified for the U.S. Olympic team in the 1500 meters and also finished fifth in the 800-meter final during the 2008 U.S. Olympic Trials. Lopez was chosen by the team captains of the U.S. Olympic team to carry the U.S. flag in the opening ceremony at the 2008 Summer Olympics in Beijing, China. The U.S. Olympians felt that he deserved the honor of flag bearer because he had overcome so many hardships and was so proud of his U.S. citizenship.

As a "Lost Boy of Sudan," Lopez overcame many challenges to survive, let alone become one of the world's top runners. His story of his race for freedom and his determination to succeed is an inspiration throughout the world.

Questions for Thought:

1. Think of the hardships that Lopez went through as a child to survive. How did that affect his determination?

2. How easy would it have been for Lopez to give up? How easily do you give up on things?

3. Lopez was elected to carry the flag because of his immense pride to be a U.S. citizen. What does pride mean to you?

Henry Marsh

Turned to the Steeplechase

Henry Marsh almost died when he was 18 months old. He was found lying face down in the goldfish pond of his grandparents' rose garden, but was revived with mouth-to-mouth resuscitation. His lungs retained some scar tissue from that accident, and that eventually led to several bouts with pneumonia. A doctor told Henry's parents that exercise would be good for him. Eventually he was the state champion in cross country in his junior and senior years of high school as well as a track and field state champion.

Henry's hero was the mile world record holder, Jim Ryun. Henry wanted to be a sub-4:00 miler like Ryun. However, when Henry went to college at Brigham Young University, the school had plenty of good milers and he wasn't even able to make the cross country team his first year. Coach Pat Shane decided to make Henry a steeplechaser and began to teach him how to hurdle. Henry's steeplechase career came to a halt when he went on a Mormon mission to Brazil. He spent two years knocking on doors, talking to people 13 hours a day, and rarely running.

Henry returned to Brigham Young for his sophomore year as a more mature man with a new attitude. His goal was to qualify for the NCAA Championships, but he needed a 30 second improvement over his best time. At the Mount Sac Relays in Walnut, California, Marsh won the race in 8:40.3, breaking the BYU record of 8:41.6 and qualifying for the NCAA Championships.

At the 1976 Olympic Trials, Henry finished second to make the U.S. Olympic team. Within the year, he had gone from being an out-of-shape missionary to an Olympian. Henry finished 10th in Montreal. The young steeplechaser continued to improve. His typical style was to run at a steady pace, usually 66 or 67 seconds per lap, stay fresh until the end, and run the last lap as fast as he could. In 1980, he ran the fastest time in the world at 8:15.68 and appeared to be in position to win an Olympic medal. However, the U.S. boycott of the 1980 Olympic Games crushed his dream.

At the 1984 Olympic Games in Los Angeles Henry was ranked second in the world, and he gave a valiant effort, but finished fourth, then collapsed to the track and was carried off on a stretcher.

The following year, he reached his boyhood dream of being a sub-4:00 miler with a 3:59.31 mile in Bern, Switzerland. He was ranked three times as the No. 1 steeplechaser in the world in 1981, 1982, and 1985. Henry set the American record four times in the steeplechase with his best of 8:09.17 in 1985.

Questions for Thought:

1. Henry's hero was Jim Ryun. Who is your hero? Why is this person your hero?

2. What characteristics should a hero have?

3. Henry wanted to be a miler like his hero, Jim Ryun, but had to switch to the steeplechase at Brigham Young University. Are you willing to try different events?

Bob Mathias

The Young Champion

Bob Mathias suffered from anemia in early childhood and had to live on special diets, take iron pills, and take frequent naps to conserve his strength. Bob overcame anemia and became a high school track star in the discus, shot put, high hurdles, high jump, and sprints. For a new challenge, his coach suggested that Bob expand his versatility and compete in the decathlon.

Bob agreed, even though he only had three weeks to prepare for the event and had never competed in the pole vault, long jump, javelin, or 1500-meter run. He won his first decathlon. In his second decathlon, he was the surprise winner of the Olympic Trials. Bob was on the U.S. Olympic team as a 17-year-old.

At the 1948 London Olympics, competing in only his third decathlon, Bob still knew little about the event. Unaware of the event rules, he nearly fouled out of the shot put and almost no-heighted in the high jump. Surprisingly, Bob was in third place after the first day. The discus was his specialty, and he responded with a big throw to move into first place. Bad weather lengthened the second day's competition to more than 12 hours. In order to conduct the javelin throw, cars were driven into the stadium with their headlights turned on to illuminate the throwing area. The final event was the 1500 meters and when a weary Bob crossed the finish line, he was the Olympic champion. Bob overcame his difficulties and in just his third decathlon, the 17-year-old had scored 7,139 points, becoming the youngest gold medalist to win a track and field event.

Bob was a talented athlete and played two seasons as a fullback at Stanford and played in the Rose Bowl. In 1952, he went to the Olympic Games in Helsinki, Finland, to defend his Olympic title. He broke his own world record, beating teammate Milt Campbell by 912 points, the largest margin in Olympic history, and became the first to successfully defend an Olympic decathlon title.

Bob Mathias went on to successful careers acting in Hollywood films, serving in the U.S. Congress, and becoming the first director of the United States Olympic Training Center.

Questions for Thought:

1. Bob won the Olympic Games in only his third decathlon. Have you had immediate success at some task? How did that affect your attitude towards the task?

2. Bob almost did not win his first Olympics because he didn't know the rules. Do you know the rules of your event? If not, what can you do to learn and understand the rules?

3. Mathias was extremely successful after his athletic career was over. How can your athletic career help your career after athletics?

Billy Mills

Believe-Believe-Believe

Photo Courtesy of Kansas Athletics

Billy Mills, a Native American (Oglala Lakota), was raised on the Pine Ridge Indian Reservation in South Dakota. He was orphaned at the age of 12. Billy took up running while attending the Haskell Institute in Lawrence, Kansas. He attended the University of Kansas and earned All-America cross country honors three times and in 1960 he won the individual title in the Big Eight cross country championship. Billy helped lead the University of Kansas track team to the 1959 and 1960 Outdoor National Championships.

Billy went on to become a lieutenant in the United States Marine Corps. After giving up running for a while, he returned to the sport to qualify for the 1964 Summer Olympics in Tokyo in the 10,000-meter run and the marathon. On October 14, 1964, 38 runners competed in the 10,000-meter final at the Tokyo Olympics. Billy had a 10,000-meter best of 29:10.4, and was a virtually unknown and not expected to be a medal contender. However, Billy, who had faced discrimination and difficult times his entire life, believed in himself. As he trained for the Olympic Games he visualized himself running the race over and over. In his mind, he saw himself running with the leaders and winning. He repeated over and over to himself the affirmation, "believe-believe-believe."

The favorite, world-record holder Ron Clarke of Australia, led most of the race with a quick pace. With one lap remaining, Clarke had dropped all his main rivals, but he still had two athletes with him. Billy Mills and Mohamed Gammoudi of Tunisia were both relatively unknown and both running much faster than they ever had before. The three were hindered by lapped runners on the last lap who made no effort to let them through on the inside. In the back straight, Clarke bumped Billy, pushing him to the outside lanes and causing him to drop back about four meters. At this point, Billy focused on his affirmations, "believe-believe-believe," as Gammoudi and Clarke sprinted for the finish. Gammoudi had shaken off Clarke and seemed to have the race won with 50 meters to go before Billy came storming past both of them to win the gold medal. Billy's winning time of 28:24.4 was a personal record by 50 seconds and a new Olympic record. The race has been called the greatest upset in Olympic history and his victory remains the only Olympic 10,000-meter win in U.S. Olympic history.

Questions for Thought:

1. Why was Billy Mills' race so surprising?

2. How did Billy prepare himself mentally to run in the Olympic Games?

3. How can you apply the story of Billy Mills to help you as an athlete and a person?

Edwin Moses

An Enduring Streak

Edwin Moses' high school basketball coach cut him from the team and the football coach kicked him off the team for fighting. He took up track and started running the hurdles and 440-yard dash. Rather than accept an athletic scholarship to a more powerful track and field program, Edwin accepted an academic scholarship in physics and engineering to Morehouse College in Atlanta, Georgia.

Edwin had run only one 400-meter hurdle race prior to running the 400-meter hurdles in March of 1976. It was only five months away from the Olympic Games in Montreal. Despite being a novice at the event, he advanced quickly. Every world class hurdler was taking 14 steps between the hurdles; however, Edwin started taking an unprecedented 13 steps between hurdles. At the Olympic Trials, Edwin won the 400-meter hurdles and set an American record with a time of 48.30.

Edwin was competing in his first international meet at the Montreal Olympics, where he won the gold, setting a world record of 47.64. His eight meter victory over U.S. teammate Mike Shine was the largest winning margin ever in that event in the Olympics. He had accomplished the extraordinary feat of becoming the 400-meter hurdles Olympic champion and world record holder in his first year of running the event. For the next decade, he dominated the 400-meter hurdles with the longest winning streak achieved by an individual athlete in track and field. Edwin was unbeatable on the track, but politics prevented him from winning his second Olympic gold when President Carter ordered the United States Olympic teams to boycott the 1980 Olympics.

At the 1984 Olympics in Los Angeles, Edwin became only the second man to win the Olympic 400-meter hurdles twice. One of the greatest honors and most memorable moments of his career came when he was chosen to recite the Athletes' Oath during the opening ceremonies in Los Angeles. He came back four years later at the 1988 Olympic Games in Seoul to finish third in the final race of his career.

Edwin was the dominant 400-meter hurdler in track and field for more than a decade. His 107 straight wins in a period of almost 10 years is the longest winning streak ever in track and field, and is considered one of the top winning streaks in all of sports. He was a strong advocate against steroid use and performance enhancing drugs. His phenomenal rise to world prominence by becoming an Olympic champion in his first year running an event was a remarkable achievement.

Questions for Thought:

1. Edwin Moses did not use being a novice as an excuse, as he won an Olympic medal only five months after first running the 400-meter hurdles. When you first begin a task, what do you focus on?

2. What are some keys to consistently performing well over a long period of time?

3. Edwin took a strong stand against the use of performance enhancing drugs. How strong is your stand against performance enhancing drugs?

Renaldo Nehemiah

The Amazing Technician

Renaldo "Skeets" Nehemiah was the dominate 110-meter hurdler in the world from 1978 until 1981, holding the world record and being the first man to run the high hurdles in under 13 seconds. Renaldo began his hurdling career in 1973 as a ninth-grader in New Jersey. He decided to try the hurdles because "everyone else was afraid of 'em." In his sophomore year of high school, Renaldo suffered a bad hamstring and glute tear, an injury that almost put an end to his career before it ever got off the ground. He did not run at all his sophomore year and spent much of his junior year recuperating, so his first full healthy season was his senior year. Renaldo trained for the 110-meter hurdles like a middle distance runner and established the legendary work ethic that would later enable him to become a dominant hurdler.

Renaldo attended the University of Maryland, where he won three NCAA titles (two of which were indoor). His sophomore year at Maryland proved to be his breakout year. He set world records twice in two weeks in the 110-meter hurdles, running 13.16 and then 13.0.

Renaldo's sophomore year at the University of Maryland ended up being his last one as an athlete there, although he continued his studies at Maryland and graduated in four years. After winning three NCAA titles, breaking the world record, and becoming the first man to run under 13.0, he turned professional.

Renaldo was the overwhelming favorite to win the 110-meter hurdles in the 1980 Summer Olympics. However, the U.S. led a 64-nation boycott of the Moscow Games. President Jimmy Carter's decision to boycott the 1980 Olympic Games in Moscow as a means of protesting Russia's occupation of Afghanistan crushed the dreams of a lot of athletes. For Renaldo, it denied him of the opportunity to reveal his technical skills on a world stage at a time when he was beginning to reach his prime.

Renaldo felt he had wasted four years of training and didn't want to risk another four years of training with the possibility of another boycott. Renaldo Nehemiah joined the NFL's San Francisco 49ers in 1982 as a wide receiver, and was a member of their 1984 Super Bowl team, although he was not a major player in their success. The Super Bowl ring did not bring him the satisfaction that an Olympic gold medal would have brought him, so he returned to track in 1986, achieving world rankings four more times before retiring from athletics after the 1991 season.

Questions for Thought:

1. Renaldo Nehemiah is known as the greatest technician ever in the hurdles. He spent many hours studying the event. How much do you study your event?

2. Renaldo's career almost ended due to injury before it started. His persistence eventually led to a world record. How persistent are you in learning a new skill?

3. Renaldo's passion for track caused him to give up football and return to track. How passionate are you about what you do?

Bill Nieder

Never Give Up

Bill Nieder threw the shot put and set the state record as a senior for Lawrence High School in Kansas. Bill was also a great football player and started his collegiate football career at the University of Kansas as a Jayhawk. His freshman year on the Kansas squad, he injured his right knee. In the hospital, his foot developed the early stages of gangrene and nearly had to be amputated. Throughout his lifetime, he continued having knee troubles with three additional surgeries and had it drained 150 times. After a long process of rehabilitation, Bill began his collegiate track career.

Despite having to use an unorthodox rotation when he threw due to his previous knee injury, Bill had a very successful career, winning the 1955 NCAA shot put title. He set collegiate records and became the first collegian to throw the shot more than 60 feet, and only the second man in history to throw more than 60 feet.

Photo Courtesy of Kansas Athletics

In the 1956 Olympics Games, Bill won the silver medal, finishing behind U.S.A. teammate Parry O'Brien. He continued to train another four years for a chance to move to the top step of the Olympic Games podium. Unfortunately, he re-injured his knee and was only able to finish fourth at the 1960 Olympic Trials, failing to qualify for the U.S. team. His Olympic dream of capturing the gold appeared to be over. He was asked to continue working out with the Olympic team and competed in three meets before the team's departure for Rome. At the first meet, he out-threw the other members of the U.S. Olympic team by a foot and a half. He won the next meet, and in the final competition, he broke his own world record with a 65-10 throw. Because of his great showing and an injury to another member of the team, he was placed on the 1960 Olympic team.

At the Olympic Games in Rome, Bill rose to the occasion. On his fifth throw, he exploded with a throw of 64-6¾, winning the competition and setting a new Olympic record. Finishing second, almost two feet behind, was the defending Olympic champion Parry O'Brien.

Bill Nieder overcame obstacle after obstacle and never gave up. His optimistic attitude and commitment paid off with an Olympic championship.

Questions for Thought:

1. When Bill finished fourth in the Olympic Trials, he worked that much harder to prove himself. When you come close to your goal, but fail to reach it, what is your reaction?

2. Do you have a physical injury that you have to overcome? How determined are you to overcome it?

3. How do you feel when you overcome obstacle after obstacle and finally achieve your goal?

David Neville

From The Outside to the Podium

David Neville stood at the 400-meter starting line in lane eight with an opportunity before him. He was not considered a favorite to finish in the top three to make the 2008 United States Olympic team that would compete in Beijing, China. The fact that he drew lane eight made it very difficult, since a runner in the far outside lane has a hard time judging the pace because they are unable to see their opponents. When the gun fired, David, in his own words, "running scared," held the lead through 300 meters. LaShawn Merritt and Jeremy Wariner both passed him, but David dug down deep within himself, laying it all on the line, and drove across the finish line to finish third. He made the Olympic team with a personal best time of 44.61. He was so physically exhausted he was unable to take the traditional victory lap taken by the top three qualifiers.

David progressed through the 400-meter qualifying rounds in Beijing and qualified for the final. The Olympic track in Beijing had nine lanes, and ironically David drew lane nine, putting him at a distinct disadvantage. Just as in Eugene at the Olympic Trials, he was not a favorite to medal and was stuck in an outside lane.

As the race progressed David said, "I didn't look behind, I didn't look back, and I just kept my eye focused on the prize that was ahead." As the runners came down the homestretch with heavy fatigue building up within their muscles, David and Bahamian Chris Brown were locked in an epic duel for the bronze medal.

David said after the race, "Sometimes we have to sacrifice our bodies, our minds, our spirits. That's what I did. I knew I had to dive." The dive earned David the Olympic bronze medal, four-one-hundredths of a second ahead of Brown. Medical attendants brought a stretcher to David, but he declined help. "Sometimes you have to sit there and take in the moment and live with the pain. That's what I did," he said. David came back to run the third leg of the U.S. 4x400 meter relay team that won gold in an Olympic record time.

David had many talents besides running. In his freshman year at Indiana University, he chose not to participate in track, but rather in the marching band as a snare drummer. David Neville overcame the odds of being an underdog and running scared from the outside lanes to become an Olympic medalist.

Questions for Thought:

1. David Neville qualified for the Olympic team by running scared. Have you competed in an event where you competed scared and the results turned out well?

2. David overcame the odds of being in the outside lanes. Have you ever felt like you were on the outside looking in? How do you successfully handle that?

3. Despite heavy fatigue, David was able to finish well by making sacrifices. What sacrifices do you make in training and in competition to be successful?

Paavo Nurmi

The Flying Finn

As an athlete, Paavo Nurmi of Finland, the "Flying Finn" was ahead of his time. Paavo had a passion for the sport of running. He trained with a dedication and intensity that had never been previously seen. He raised the quantity and quality of endurance training to levels that none of his contemporaries could equal. His competitive fires burned with a will to succeed in life. Running was his way to meet the high standards he set for himself.

Paavo's first Olympic race was in Antwerp, Belgium, in 1920 at 5000 meters and ended in defeat to Joseph Guillemot of France. This was to be the only time that Paavo lost in an Olympic final to a foreign runner. Just days later, he won gold medals at 10,000 meters, individual cross country, and team cross country (cross country is no longer an Olympic sport).

Paavo meticulously planned his workouts using his stopwatch to time his training. His focus was not on his competition, but on achieving a certain pace. His guiding principle was, "When you race against time, you don't have to sprint. Others can't hold the pace if it is steady and hard all through to the tape."

Going into the 1924 Olympics in Paris, Paavo held the world records in three events: the mile, 5000 meters, and 10,000 meters, a feat no one else in history has been able to accomplish. The 1924 Olympic Games in Paris was the finest hour for the Finnish athlete. Paavo won five gold medals in six days, winning the 1500 and the 5000 meters with less than two hours between the two finals. He also won the cross country race and led Finland to gold medals in the cross country team competition and the 3000 meter team race.

On a tour of the United States in 1925, Paavo raced 55 times in five months, losing only one time. By the 1928 Olympics in Amsterdam, Paavo was 31 years of age. He won gold in the 10,000 meters and silver in both the 5000 meters and the 3000-meter steeplechase. More determined than ever, Paavo trained hard for his fourth Olympic Games to be held in Los Angeles in 1932. His greatest ambition was to crown his career with a gold medal in the Olympic marathon. Unfortunately, the International Amateur Athletic Federation suspended Paavo from international competition following accusations of professionalism. His legacy consists of 25 world records and 12 Olympic medals in track and field.

Questions for Thought:

1. Paavo Nurmi revolutionized training with his pace work. Think about the training methods you use and how they make you successful.

2. Paavo had a passion for running and training. How does having passion help you to become better? What are some things you could do to help capture the passion?

3. How do you handle fatigue, physically and mentally, if you have multiple events in a competition?

Dan O'Brien

World's Greatest Athlete

Photo Courtesy of USATF

Dan O'Brien was born in Portland, Oregon, where his parents gave him up for adoption at birth. Dan was talented, but lacked commitment to develop his skills. Eventually, Dan made the commitment to be the "best athlete in the world" and turned to the decathlon. Coached by Mike Keller and Rick Sloan, Dan improved to become a top decathlete.

Dan set the world record in the decathlon and was favored to win the Olympic gold medal in 1992. Reebok created a popular TV advertising campaign featuring U.S. rivals Dave Johnson and Dan. The commercials, entitled "Dan & Dave," were meant to build interest in Reebok and the decathletes, culminating in the 1992 Summer Olympics in Barcelona. However, at the 1992 U.S. Olympic Trials in New Orleans, Dan, seeking to conserve his energy in the hot and humid conditions, passed on the lower heights in the pole vault. When he entered the competition at 15-9, he failed in his first two attempts at his opening height. Dan was down to one more jump. Unfortunately, he missed on his third and final attempt, resulting in no points for the event and he did not qualify for the Olympic team. His unexpected failure caused Reebok to revise new ads featuring Dan cheering on Dave, who went on to win the bronze medal.

Dan went to work the next four years to prepare for the 1996 Olympic Games in Atlanta. Dan won all eight decathlons he entered, won two world championships by impressive margins, and set a world record of 8,891 points. For Dan to win the 1996 Olympics, he had to qualify for the U.S. team. This was a challenge he had failed at in the last Olympic Trials. The ghosts of failure were on his mind as he stood on the pole vault runway at the 1996 Olympic Trials in Atlanta. With his 15-foot fiberglass pole, he ran down the runway, planted his pole, and soared over the bar. His failure at the 1992 Trials was behind him.

Under intense pressure of competing in his home country as the world record holder, he rose to the challenge, earning the title as "the world's greatest athlete" as he captured the decathlon gold at the 1996 Summer Olympics in Atlanta, Georgia.

Questions for Thought:

1. Dan failed to make the team in 1992 and had nightmares about the miss. Eventually, he put it out of his mind to be successful. How do you forget about past mistakes?

2. It took Dan a while before he eventually made a commitment to use his talent. How can you make a commitment to use the talent you have?

3. How can a failure motivate you?

Al Oerter

Competitor

Photo Courtesy of Kansas Athletics

The word that best describes Al Oerter is "competitor." He is the only athlete to win four gold medals at four successive Olympiads and set four consecutive Olympic records. At Sewanhaka High School in New York, he was a sprinter and then a miler. As he was running at practice one day, a discus landed near his feet. He picked it up and casually threw it back. His coach noticed that he threw it back farther than the discus throwers were throwing it. So, Al became a discus thrower. He set the national high school record, and then attended the University of Kansas, where he won two NCAA titles. While at Kansas, Al competed in his first Olympics at the 1956 Summer Games in Melbourne. He was not considered the favorite, but won gold after he unleashed a throw of 184-11, which was a personal best and Olympic record.

An automobile accident at the age of 20 nearly killed him, but he recovered in time to compete at the 1960 Summer Olympics in Rome. Al threw the discus 194-2, setting an Olympic record and winning his second gold medal. During the early 1960s, Al continued to have success, setting his first world record in 1962 as he became the first man to throw more than 200 feet in the discus. He was considered a heavy favorite to win a third gold medal in Tokyo in 1964. However, he was bothered by a neck injury, and six days before the competition, he slipped on a wet concrete discus circle and tore rib cartilage on his throwing side, causing internal bleeding and severe pain. Team doctors told him not to throw for six weeks. He refused. "These are the Olympics," he was quoted as saying at the time. "You die before you quit." Competing in great pain, Al set a new Olympic record and won a third Olympic gold medal.

Al returned to the Olympics in 1968 at Mexico City. However, experts felt that at age 32, he was too old to win. Rising to the occasion, as he always did in the Olympic Games, Al released another personal record and another Olympic record throw of 212-6 to win and become the first track and field athlete to win four consecutive gold medals. Al Oerter retired from athletics after the 1968 Olympics. He did make an attempt to qualify for the American team in 1980 at the age of 43, but he finished fourth, one spot from making the Olympic team. However, he did set his overall personal record of 227-10¾ that year.

Questions for Thought:

1. Al Oerter rose to the occasion to set a personal record in every Olympic Games he competed in. What is the key to rising to the occasion?

2. Al threw in severe pain instead of quitting. On a scale of 1-10, (10 high) what is your pain tolerance?

3. At the age of 43, Al achieved a new personal record. How do you maintain that high of a performance level for that long?

Jesse Owens

The Buckeye Bullet

Jesse Owens was the seventh of 11 children. His father was a sharecropper and his grandfather was a slave. At East Technical High School in Cleveland, Jesse tied the national high school record of 9.4 in the 100-yard dash, set new national high school records in the 220-yard dash and long jump.

Jesse attended Ohio State University, but in order to make ends meet he worked several jobs as an elevator operator, a waiter, and pumped gas to support himself and his young wife, Ruth. One of the greatest sporting achievements ever occurred at the Big 10 Championships in Ann Arbor, Michigan, on May 25, 1935. After falling down a flight of stairs a few days before the meet, Jesse was uncertain that he would even be able to compete, but decided to take it one event at a time. In just 45 minutes, Jesse set three world records and tied a fourth in the 100-yard dash, 220-yard dash, 220-yard hurdles, and the long jump. The long jump record would last for 25 years. Jesse won a record four gold medals in the 1935 NCAA Championships and duplicated the feat the following year.

Jesse's phenomenal success at Ohio State gave him confidence that he could compete at the world level. The 1936 Olympics were held in Nazi Germany. In a remarkable display of athletic ability, Jesse became the first track and field athlete to win four gold medals in a single Olympiad. At a time when segregation was deep rooted, Jesse's performance discredited Hitler's master race theory. After the 100 meters, he was struggling in the long jump. He had one remaining jump left to attempt to make the final when German Luz Long gave him some helpful advice in marking his takeoff point, which enabled him to win the event. Long and Jesse would remain lifelong friends. The next day, he won the 200 meters and then anchored the 4x100-meter relay team to a gold medal. The founder of Adidas, Adi Dassler, gave Jesse Adidas shoes, marking the first sponsorship for a male African-American athlete. Despite Hitler's attitude, the Germans considered Jesse a hero, cheering loudly for him and seeking his autograph. Jesse was even allowed to travel with and stay in the same hotel as whites, which was not happening in the United States at that time.

Jesse worked with youth, sharing himself and the little material wealth that he had. He was a champion on the playground in the poorest neighborhoods as much as he was on the oval of the Olympic Games. 1981, the Jesse Owens Award was established by USA Track and Field. The award is regarded as the highest accolade, presented annually to the outstanding U.S. male and female performers.

Questions for Thought:

1. Despite being injured, Jesse set four world records in one day. What do you focus on when you have an injury bothering you?

2. Luz Long, a competitor, gave Jesse advice that eventually led to Jesse defeating Long. On a scale of 1-10 (10 high), how is your sportsmanship?

3. Jesse never accumulated much money, but gave freely to others. Are you a rich person in areas other than money?

Eulace Peacock

Glory Denied

Eulace Peacock was born in Dothan, Alabama, but moved to New Jersey as a small child. He started his track career as an 11-year-old, jumping 15-0 in the long jump. By the time Peacock graduated from high school in 1934, he had become a high school legend. He set records of 9.7 for the 100-yard dash, 21.7 for the 220-yard dash, and 24-4½ for the long jump.

Eulace rejected numerous track and field scholarships in favor of a football scholarship to Temple University. It was his dream to play college football under the famous Temple coach, Glenn "Pop" Warner, but fear of injury before the 1936 Olympic Games in Berlin kept him off the gridiron.

Eulace's major rival was Jesse Owens. Owens had set four world records in one day at the Big 10 Conference track meet in 1935. However, for the remainder of 1935, Eulace Peacock dominated Jesse Owens, defeating him in seven of their 10 meetings in the sprints and long jump. At the 1935 National Amateur Athletic Union Outdoor Championships in Lincoln, Nebraska, Eulace defeated his famous rival in both the 100-meter dash and in the long jump. It was Eulace, not Jesse Owens, who appeared to be the world's greatest sprinter and long jumper at the time.

Bad luck struck in Milan, Italy, in 1935, when Eulace suffered a hamstring pull. He attempted to come back and appeared poised for glory in the 1936 Olympic Games. However, when running in the 1936 Penn Relays, he aggravated the same hamstring pull. The injury cost him a place on the Olympic team and forever ruined his dreams of Olympic glory.

Jesse Owens, in a historic performance, would go on to win four gold medals in the Berlin Olympics and become an American legend. Had it not been for the hamstring injury, the fate of history may have made Eulace the American legend.

After graduating from Temple in 1937, Eulace served with the U.S. Coast Guard in World War II for four years. He continued to excel at track and field, winning national championships and long jumping more than 26 feet. Denied of an opportunity to excel in the Olympics because of the hamstring injury, Eulace was denied again in 1940 and 1944 when the Olympics were cancelled due to World War II.

Questions for Thought:

1. Few people have heard of Eulace Peacock, even though he consistently beat Jesse Owens. How do you handle it when you don't get the recognition you deserve?

2. Eulace never got an opportunity to compete in the Olympics. How do you take advantage of the opportunities that you have?

3. What is your frame of mind like when you compete against someone that is perceived to be better than you

Dorando Pietri

I will win or I will die

Before the London Olympics in 1908, the marathon event was an even 26 miles. Officials at the London Olympics wanted the 26-mile journey to end in front of the feet of the Queen of England in the grandstands, so they extended the course 365 yards. That extra 365 yards would prove to be crucial for Dorando Pietri of Italy.

Dorando thought the field had gone out too fast, but he stayed close to the leaders and gradually worked himself into the lead. As Dorando reached the entrance of the stadium where nearly a hundred thousand spectators were awaiting his arrival, his effort had left him totally exhausted. His lips moved as if in prayer repeating over and over the mantra, "Vincerò o morirò," "I will win or I will die." As he began to enter the stadium, he fell, but in a short time he recovered sufficiently to enter the stadium.

"You're nearly there, you're nearly there," officials told him as he staggered down the slope on to the running track. He turned to the right and heard, "Wrong way, wrong way." He collapsed on the track. Officials picked him up. Only his dry lips, caked with salt and sweat, moved silently saying, "I will win or I will die". He got up again and seemed to have no idea where he was or what he was doing. He shuffled forward, every tottering step now was bringing him closer to the finish line. Behind him, John Hayes of the United States, having paced himself to stay fresh, was moving up fast. Dorando managed to finish the race and then collapsed again for the last time. All eyes were on the fallen Dorando when Hayes crossed the finish line. Dorando was unconscious as he was placed on a stretcher and carried off the track.

The British judges debated for over an hour before announcing that Dorando had been disqualified for receiving assistance, and the winner of the gold medal was John Hayes of the United States.

In defeat, Dorando's fame far exceeded that of the winner. He turned professional shortly after the 1908 Olympics and enjoyed a successful career in America and Europe. He eventually died of a heart attack at the age of 56 as the "wrong way" participant in one of the most famous finishes in Olympic history.

Questions for Thought:

1. Dorando was committed to finish. Think of a time when you showed a tremendous commitment.

2. Dorando went out fast and suffered. How important is it to pace yourself? How do you properly prepare yourself to do that?

3. Why did Dorando become more famous for his second place finish than Hayes did for winning?

Steve Prefontaine

A Work of Art

Photo Courtesy of USATF

During his brief 24-year life, Steve Prefontaine grew from hometown hero, to record-setting college phenomenon, to internationally acclaimed track star. Since his death in 1975, Pre has become a legend. He combined talent, discipline (he never missed a workout in four years of college), and determination with a personality that gained him many fans who came to watch him run, roaring with cheers of "Go Pre!"

Pre developed his hunger to be the best at Marshfield High School in Coos Bay, Oregon. As a freshman at Marshfield High School, he placed 53rd in the state cross country meet. Prefontaine ran a personal best time of 5:01 in the mile his freshman year. Determined to improve, Pre undertook a high mileage training plan during the summer and the following year, he placed sixth in the state cross country meet. However, in his sophomore track and field season, he failed to qualify for state. Motivated, he continued to train hard and his junior and senior years proved highly successful. He won every meet, including the state meet, and set a national high school record his senior year in the two mile race with a time of 8:41.5.

Pre ran for the University of Oregon and won three NCAA Cross Country Championships and four straight three-mile titles in track and field. Following his freshman year, he went undefeated. He was known for going out hard and not relinquishing the lead, a tactic that his fans and fellow competitors admired.

He set the American record at 5000 meters during the 1972 Olympic Games in Munich. Pre led nearly the entire last mile in a fierce battle with Lasse Viren of Finland, but was passed with 150 meters to go and finished fourth.

Before his tragic death in a car accident in 1975, Prefontaine held every American record from the 2,000 meters to the 10,000 meters. He is considered one of the greatest American runners of all time.

Questions for Thought:

1. What made Pre such a great runner?

2. Years after his death, Pre is still considered a legend. Why?

3. What do you think is the most admirable quality Pre possessed?

Famous Quotes by Steve Prefontaine:

A lot of people run a race to see who is fastest. I run to see who has the most guts, who can punish himself into an exhausting pace, and then at the end, punish himself even more. Nobody is going to win a 5000 meter race after running an easy 2 miles. Not with me. If I lose forcing the pace all the way, well, at least I can live with myself.

To give anything less than your best is to sacrifice the gift.

I don't just go out there and run. I like to give people watching something exciting. Somebody may beat me, but they are going to have to bleed to do it.

I'm going to work so that it's a pure guts race at the end, and if it is, I am the only one who can win it.

How does a kid from Coos Bay, with one leg longer than the other win races? All my life people have been telling me, 'You're too small Pre', 'You're not fast enough Pre.' 'Give up your foolish dream Steve.' But they forgot something. I have to win.

A race is a work of art that people can look at and be affected in as many ways they're capable of understanding.

Bob Richards

Pole Vaulting Parson

Bob Richards participated in diving and tumbling before starting to pole vault in junior high school. He played quarterback in high school before attending the University of Illinois. After his parents divorced, he was reared by a minister.

Bob began his Olympic career in the 1948 Olympics in London. At the age of 22, he finished third in the pole vault. That was only the beginning of a great career.

By 1952, Bob had established himself as one of the top pole vaulters in the world and one of only two vaulters who had cleared the magic height of 15 feet. At this time pole vaulters used bamboo poles and jumping 15-0 was considered a magic barrier. At the U.S. Olympic Trials, he made the team but he suffered a pulled muscle while vaulting. By the time the U.S. team arrived in Helsinki, Finland, for the Olympics, Bob wasn't even sure he would be able to compete. Miraculously, his leg was feeling better the day of the Olympic final. With the bar raised to 14-11, only two men remained in the competition and both missed their first two attempts. Bob raced down the runway on his final attempt, planted his bamboo pole, and pushed up and over. He had won the Olympic gold and set a new Olympic record of 14-11.

Four years later in the 1956 Melbourne Olympics, he was the overwhelming favorite but again had an injury. Starting two feet lower than normal, he missed his first two attempts. On the brink of elimination, on his final jump, he cleared the height. He went on to win his second Olympic gold and set an Olympic record of 14-11½. In 1958 Bob became the first athlete to appear on the front of the Wheaties cereal box.

In 1960 he made his fourth Olympic team, this time as a decathlete and finished 13th in the competition. He became an ordained minister and was one of the first participants in masters track and field.

Questions for Thought:

1. Bob used bamboo poles to vault. How has equipment changed over the years to help performance?

2. Bob put his injury in the back of his mind to win a gold medal. How do you shift your focus from the negative to the positive?

3. Bob was the second man ever over the magic 15-0 barrier. Do you believe barriers are more physical or mental?

Derek Redmond

Determined to Finish

Derek Redmond, of Great Britain, arrived at the 1992 Summer Olympic Games in Barcelona determined to win a medal. Although he did not achieve his goal, his performance over 400 meters became one of the most inspiring performances in Olympic history.

Derek first started a successful track career in Great Britain at the age of 7. It didn't take him long to become the British champion and record holder at 400 meters. He set the British record for the 400-meter run at the age of 19 when he ran 44.82, which he later improved to 44.50. However, injuries consistently plagued Derek's career. He had 13 operations on his Achilles tendons and knees and it forced him to pull out of many major competitions. In the 1988 Games in Seoul, South Korea, he was forced to withdraw just 10 minutes before the race because of an Achilles injury.

The 1992 Olympics were Derek's stage and it was his time to shine and show the world his remarkable talent. Derek came into the Barcelona Games as the British record holder and in the best shape of his life. In the first round, he ran the fastest time of all the runners in the field. In the semifinal, his dad, Jim, sat in the stands supporting Derek as he did at all his competitions. As the gun sounded for the race, Derek started well and quickly took the lead. In the backstretch at the 200-meter mark, he appeared to be a lock to make the finals. Suddenly, he heard a loud pop in his right hamstring, as if he had been shot. His momentum kept him hobbling until he fell to the ground in pain. Painfully, he arose and with his leg quivering, he began to hop on one leg before falling to the track. Medical personnel ran to assist him.

Derek's Olympic dream of winning a medal was once again gone. With tears streaming down his face, Derek waved off the stretcher offered by the medical crew. He struggled to get to his feet and started hobbling down the track, the pain and agony etched deeply in his face. Derek was going to finish, not for the crowd, but for himself. One painful step at a time, Redmond limped toward the finish line. Derek's father raced down from the top of the stands to help his son, dodging security who tried to stop him.

When Jim reached his son, Derek put an arm around his father for support and the two of them slowly made their way around the track to the finish line. The full stadium of 65,000 spectators, cheering, clapping, and crying, rose to give the Redmonds a standing ovation. Derek's determination to finish the race has become one of the most inspiring races in Olympic history.

Questions for Thought:

1. Have you ever almost quit something because it was hard, but with determination, you carried on?

2. How does it feel when you reach an accomplishment that you almost gave up on?

3. Derek Redmond's father was there to help him finish. Who is on your support staff? How do they help you reach your goals?

Henry Rono

World Record Machine

Born into the Nandi Tribe in Kenya, Henry Rono was a warrior. Starting in 1977, he attended Washington State University and became only the third person in history (after Gerry Lindgren and Steve Prefontaine) to win the NCAA Men's Cross Country Championship three times, winning in 1976, 1977, and 1979. He also won multiple NCAA titles in track and field.

The peak of Henry's running career was the 1978 season. In 81 days in the summer of 1978, as a sophomore at Washington State University, Henry set four world records and dominated the sport of track and field. He broke records at 10,000 meters (27:22.5), 5000 meters (13:08.4), the 3000-meter steeplechase (8:05.4), and the 3000 meters (7:32.1); an achievement unparalleled in the history of distance running. Henry accomplished it by running out front by himself, without challengers or rabbits to push him. He set the 5000-meter world record in a dual meet and set the steeplechase world record before a crowd of 200 people.

Henry continued to run and compete at a high level for the next four years; however, he would never get to compete at the Olympics, as his country boycotted both the 1976 and the 1980 Olympic Games. Kenya's boycotts robbed Henry of a world stage and enduring fame. Kenyan track and government officials made many demands of him and took much of his newfound wealth. He had no financial manager, no investments, and little control over his money.

In the years that would follow, Henry faced far greater challenges in life than running around a track. As his problems increased, he began drinking heavily. His successes became more sporadic and he gained weight. He was soon penniless, spending time in a homeless shelter and in and out of rehabilitation clinics.

Henry Rono, the warrior, summoned the determination and courage that made him a world record holder and recovered from his alcoholism to coach at the high school level and resume running.

Questions or Thought:

1. Henry Rono set many world records in one summer. How does it feel when you are on the top of your game?

2. Henry had the capability to push himself even without challengers. He ran to get the most out of himself. Do you challenge yourself? How can you get the most out of yourself?

3. Henry overcame his personal challenges. Do your experiences in athletics help you to overcome personal challenges?

Jim Ryun

In Quest of Gold

Photo Courtesy of Kansas Athletics

As a sophomore at Wichita East High School in Kansas, Jim Ryun ran his first race, placing second in the mile run with a time of 4:32.4. The following year, in 1964, the 17-year-old junior became the first high school runner to break the four-minute barrier when he ran 3:59.0. Jim went on to qualify for the Tokyo Olympics that year as a junior in high school. As a senior, Jim won his third state title in the mile with a time of 3:58.3. Six weeks later, Jim defeated Olympic champion Peter Snell and set the American mile record in 3:55.3.

As a freshman at the University of Kansas, Jim set his first world record in the 880-yard run with a time of 1:44.9. On July 17, 1966, he ran the mile in 3:51.3, smashing the world record by 2.3 seconds. He was named Sportsman of the Year (the youngest ever) by Sports Illustrated in 1966 and won the Sullivan Award as the nation's top amateur athlete. In 1967, Jim lowered his mile record to 3:51.1, and added world records in the 1500 meters by running 3:33.1, the indoor half-mile at 1:48.3, and anchored KU's sprint medley relay team to a world record of 3:15.2.

Jim entered the 1968 Olympic Games in the high altitude of Mexico City as the world record holder and overwhelming favorite in the 1500 meters. However, earlier that summer he contracted mononucleosis and was also trying to recover from a hamstring injury. Kip Keino of Kenya bolted to an early lead and Ryun was unable to catch him, but he still won the silver medal.

Jim was not one to shy away from hard work. His grueling workout regime became folklore, with twice-a-day workouts, including up to 20 quarter-mile intervals at top speed with short rest periods. He logged 85 to 100 miles per week as a high school senior, and pushed that volume to 120 miles leading up to the 1972 Olympic Trials.

In 1972, Jim was back, making his third Olympic team to compete at the Munich Olympic Games. In a 1500-meter qualifying heat, he was tripped and fell down. By the time he got up and started running again, he was unable to qualify. Jim Ryun became one of the greatest middle distance runners of all time through hard work and talent. He can look back proudly on his accomplishments and, despite his Olympic disappointment; know that he gave everything he had as a competitor.

Questions for Thought:

1. What do you think was Jim Ryun's greatest accomplishment?

2. What would you do if you worked hard at something and it did not turn out like you had hoped?

3. Can you say that you have given everything you have as a competitor?

Alberto Salazar

Marathon Man

Alberto Salazar was a high school standout in Massachusetts before he attended the University of Oregon. Running for the tradition-rich Oregon Ducks, he won numerous All-American honors, a national cross country individual championship and helped his team win a national championship. In 1980, he finished third in the Olympic Trials to make the 1980 Olympic team that was to compete in Moscow. However, due to the United States' boycott, he was unable to compete. He held the American indoor 5000-meter record and was also the U.S. national cross country champion in 1979, faring well at the IAAF World Cross Country Championships, finishing second in 1982 and fourth in 1983.

Despite great success in cross country and on the track, Alberto's greatest successes came in the marathon. Alberto was known for being mentally tough. At the 1978 Falmouth Road Race, after fading to 10th place, he collapsed at the finish with a temperature of 107 degrees and was read his last rites prematurely. From 1980 to 1982, Alberto won three consecutive New York City Marathons. In his first-ever marathon, the 1980 New York City Marathon, he won in 2:09:41, which was the fastest American debut and the second-fastest time recorded by a U.S. runner at the time. The next year in 1981, Alberto set an apparent world record at the New York City Marathon of 2:08:13. However, a re-measurement of the course found it to be about 148 meters short.

In 1982, he won his first and only Boston Marathon after the famous "Duel in the Sun" with Dick Beardsley. Alberto won the race in an exciting sprint finish and collapsed at the end before being taken to an emergency room and given six liters of fluid intravenously.

Soon after the "Duel in the Sun," his athletic performance gradually declined to the point at which he could barely jog. He fell into a "more-is-better" mindset, which led him to reason that if 120 miles per week yielded a certain level of success, then 200 miles would bring even better results. The extremely long distances ultimately led to a breakdown of his immune system and he was unable to continue training. He was later diagnosed with anemia. In 1984, Alberto was a member of the United States' Olympic Marathon team and was considered a favorite to win, but he finished a disappointing 15th in 2:14:19 in the hot Los Angeles sun.

After several years of inactivity, Alberto Salazar won the prestigious 90 km (56 mile) Comrades Marathon in South Africa in 1994. He stayed connected with the sport of track and field as coach of the Nike Oregon Project, which is aimed at producing Olympic-caliber athletes.

Questions for Thought:

1. How do you prepare to compete in hot weather?

2. Alberto had a "more is better" mindset at one time. Do you believe more is better?

3. Alberto has stayed connected to the sport as a coach. Do you plan to stay connected to your sport? How will you do so?

Viktor Saneyev

Taking A Stand

Viktor Saneyev, of the Soviet Union, competed in track and field for six years before he decided to specialize in the triple jump. His first Olympic success was at the 1968 Mexico City Olympics, where he won the first of three triple jump gold medals. At the high altitude of Mexico City, the air is thinner. The thin air means less oxygen for distance runners and therefore, slower times. For sprinters and jumpers, the thin air means less air resistance and being able to jump farther. With the aid of a tailwind, four jumpers broke world records before Viktor soared 57-0¾ to clinch the gold. Viktor continued to dominate the triple jump event during the late 1960s and 1970s. Four years after he first set the world record, he broke it again, increasing it to 57-2¾. He won the triple jump again at the 1972 Olympic Games in Munich and entered the 1976 Olympic Games in Montreal as the favorite. However, he was bothered by a nagging Achilles injury. Despite the injury, Viktor rose to meet the challenge, coming from behind in the final rounds to win his third gold medal.

The 1970s was an era when many Soviet and East German athletes took performance enhancing drugs. Viktor courageously spoke out against such use. He stood firmly against the use of illegal performance enhancing drugs and denounced all drug use. He even refused his wife's attempts to give him vitamin supplements.

At the 1980 Moscow Olympics, Viktor should have won his fourth consecutive Olympic gold medal, but was involved in a controversial triple jump officiating fiasco, and had to settle for the silver medal. Film evidence supported Viktor's claim that he jumped farther than the eventual winner.

In terms of Olympic gold medals, Viktor's three consecutive Olympic victories in one event stands behind only discus champion Al Oerter and Carl Lewis in the long jump, each with four consecutive Olympic gold medals in one event.

In 1991, Victor was struck head-on by a drunk driver and after a nine-month battle, had to have his right leg amputated below the knee.

Questions for Thought:

1. Viktor took the path less traveled and stood for what was right in terms of drug use. Do you stand for what is right even though it may not be popular?

2. Viktor believed the use of performance enhancing drugs was cheating. He liked to win the right way. What is winning the right way?

3. Viktor had the determination to take a stand against drug use. What does determination mean to you?

Wes Santee

The Race for Sub-4:00

Wes Santee, one of the world's greatest distance runners in the 1950s, narrowly missed becoming the first man to run the mile under 4:00. Wes grew up on the western plains of Ashland, Kansas, where he ran for fun. As a sophomore at the University of Kansas he earned a spot on the 1952 Olympic team. Even though he was the fastest miler in the world, Wes was not allowed to run the 1500 meters (metric mile) in the 1952 Olympic Games because of a controversial decision by the U.S. Olympic Committee, who decided he would run the 5000 meters instead. Wes finished a disappointing 13th in his qualifying heat at the Olympics and did not make the final of the 5000-meter run.

After the Olympic Games, Wes boldly announced he would be the first runner to break the 4:00 mark in the mile run. Wes, along with Roger Bannister of Great Britain and John Landy of Australia, were in a race to see who would be the first to break the magical four-minute barrier. As history indicates, it was Roger Bannister of Great Britain who accomplished that goal on May 6, 1954. Wes followed a short time later with a two-week stretch that saw him run the next three fastest miles ever recorded, including a 4:00.5 clocking. Wes won numerous national titles and broke Glenn Cunningham's world record for the indoor mile, but never was able to accomplish his sub-4 minute mile goal.

Wes was a versatile runner and a true team player. He ran numerous anchor legs for many of the University of Kansas relay teams. He was a NCAA Cross Country Champion and was named the outstanding athlete at the Drake, Kansas, and Texas Relays. He often ran several races in the same meet, which may have had a cumulative fatigue effect and hindered him in his effort to be the first to break the 4:00 mile.

Although Wes Santee was not the first man to break four minutes for the mile, his pursuit of the magic sub-4:00 mile barrier made him a running legend.

Questions for Thought:

1. How do you feel when you come tantalizingly close to accomplishing a goal, but just miss it?

2. Does failure motive you to do better?

3. Wes gave up an opportunity for a possible sub-4:00 mile to help his team. What have you given up or are willing to give up to help your teammates?

Steve Scott

America's Mile Legend

Steve Scott's father was an overweight physician who smoked and did not see the value of running. However, Steve's mother was a runner before the running boom made running popular in the United States. Steve watched U.S. runner Dave Wottle win the 800-meter gold medal in the 1972 Olympics on television, wearing his famous golf cap. Wottle's win and cap inspired Steve, so he wore a cap in every race of his 1972 cross country season. In his junior year of high school, Steve made the varsity cross country squad as the fifth runner, running the 800 meters in 1:58 and the mile in 4:30. By his senior year, Steve became the top runner on his cross country team and improved his track times to 1:52 in the 800 meters and 4:15 in the mile.

Steve attended the University of California, Irvine and was a four-time NCCA Champion. He ran his first sub-4:00 mile indoors his junior year in college. From his start as an unknown college runner, until the time he graduated from college, he ran 11 sub-4:00 miles. Steve quickly became the top miler in the United States and won the 1500 meters at the 1980 U.S. Olympic Trials, but did not compete at the Moscow Olympic Games due to the U.S. boycott. At the 1984 Olympic Games in Los Angeles, he placed 10th and in the 1988 Games in Seoul, he was fifth in the 1500 meters.

Steve's greatest legacy was setting three American mile records. He became the first American to break 3:50 in the mile, with a time of 3:49.68. He later ran 3:47.69, the second-fastest mile in history at the time, and an American record that would stand for more than a quarter of a century. He ran 136 sub-4:00 miles in his career, more than any other runner in history.

In training, Steve ran several miles every morning followed by an intense track workout in the evening. On the weekend, he ran long runs as far as 20 miles. He routinely exceeded 100 miles per week.

Steve's attempt to run a sub-4:00 mile at age 40 in 1994 was derailed by a battle with his most formidable opponent, cancer. His recovery from testicular cancer and return to masters competition demonstrated that the powerful force of will, more than physical ability, is the true mark of a champion.

Questions for Thought:

1.   Steve did not start out as the top runner on his cross country team, but eventually set the American record in the mile. What is the key to improving that much?

2.   Steve never won a medal at the Olympics, but was one of the top milers in the world for years. What is more important to you, winning medals or performing up to your potential?

3.   Do you believe that will is more important than talent?

Bob Schul

Lone American 5000-Meter Olympic Champion

Bob Schul was raised on a farm in West Milton, Ohio. Despite having asthma, a condition he battled throughout his career, he started running in the seventh grade and ran a 4:34.5 mile in high school. He attended Miami University in Ohio and immediately began to improve his running times, clocking a 4:12.1 mile as a sophomore.

Bob joined the Air Force and was introduced to Hungarian coach Mihaly Igloi. Under Igloi's training he finished third at the U.S. National Championships in the 3000-meter steeplechase. In 1962, he contracted mononucleosis and spent three months in an Air Force hospital, but recovered the following year. While competing for Miami University of Ohio, he broke the American record for three miles and then the American record for 5000 meters, running 13:38.

He won the 1964 U.S. Olympic Trials 5000 meters and entered the 1964 Olympics in Tokyo with the best time in the world. In Japan, the final was held in heavy rain. Known for his devastating kick, Bob overcame a 10-meter deficit on the back stretch, running a 54.8 last lap that none of the other runners could match. In capturing the gold medal, he became the only American ever to have won the Olympic 5000 meters.

After the 1964 Olympics, Bob suffered a multitude of injuries. He never returned to his 1964 Olympic form, but he did qualify for the Olympic Trials in 1968 and made a valiant attempt to make the Olympic team. He had an asthma attack a few laps into the race and struggled throughout, passing out as he crossed the finish line.

Questions for Thought:

1. Bob overcame a lifelong struggle with asthma to be successful. How have you overcome any medical challenges?

2. Bob won the Olympics with a devastating kick. What contributes to being able to finish strong?

3. How can you develop a stronger finish?

Bob Seagren

Rising to the Top

Bob Seagren learned to pole vault as a teenager in California by jumping from rooftop to rooftop on bamboo poles he picked up from a rug store. He graduated from rooftops to become a four-time NCAA champion for the University of Southern California and claimed the world record in the pole vault in 1966.

Bob participated in his first Olympic Games in 1968 in Mexico City. He surprised everyone by passing when the bar was at 17-6½. Bob was unfamiliar with the metric system used in international competition, and he thought that 5.35 meters (actually 17-6½) was relatively low. In an exciting back and forth contest, the top three vaulters all cleared the same height of 17-8½ and Bob won the gold medal because he had the fewest misses.

A knee injury and operation sidelined him from competition for a year and a half. While he was out of action, the world record was raised several times. Bob came back as determined as ever to reclaim the world record and became the first American to vault over 18 feet.

Bob was involved in a controversy at the 1972 Olympics. He had vaulted a world best 18-5¾ that year using a carbon pole. The International Amateur Athletic Federation (I.A.A.F.) ruled that the pole was illegal shortly before the Olympics. Bob and other vaulters protested and the ban was lifted four days before competition was to begin. However, the night before the qualifying round, the IAAF once again implemented the ban and the illegal poles were confiscated. Forced to vault with an unfamiliar pole, Bob managed to win a silver medal with a vault of 17-8½. East German Wolfgang Nordwig, who was able to use his familiar vaulting pole, won the gold medal. It was the first time an American had failed to win the Olympic gold medal in the pole vault.

Bob Seagren went on to become an actor, appearing in several movies and television shows.

Questions for Thought:

1. When Bob was injured he saw several people surpass his world record. If you are injured and see other people performing better than you, what should you focus on?

2. When the I.A.A.F. made a last second ruling and deprived Bob of the vaulting pole he had practiced on, it made it difficult to adapt. How do you adapt to the changing environment around you?

3. Bob Seagren had a successful athletic career and then a successful professional career. What do you plan to do after your athletic career is over?

Ryan Shay

Living Life to the Fullest

Running is typically viewed as an individual sport, but Ryan Shay displayed the team aspect of cross country competition at the 2001 Big East Cross Country Championships. Ryan entered his final cross country season at Notre Dame as a favorite to win the NCAA cross country title, but an injury to his Achilles tendon put him in an air-cast boot. A lingering illness had also taken him out of his training. Ryan was barely able to walk, much less run. He had only been training for five days and he knew that he would not be able to perform up to his own high standards. But he knew that he still could help the team, so he ran the meet on his bad leg and helped Notre Dame win the Big East cross country title.

Joe Piane, his distance coach at Notre Dame, stated, "The hardest thing to do as a coach was hold Ryan back. He also was a great leader and team captain. He would not stand for anyone else on the team running poorly." As a student he was an Academic All-American.

Ryan entered the 10,000-meter race in the 2001 NCAA Track and Field Championships as the No. 4 seed, but he made a bold, determined move and took the lead after the first lap. By the time Shay reached the halfway mark, the race had become a two-man battle between himself and Murray Link of Arkansas. A tenacious Ryan would dominate the field by leading the final 24 laps to win. It was his ninth All-American honor at Notre Dame.

After graduating from college, Ryan turned his attention to the marathon and won the 2003 U.S. Marathon Championships, becoming that event's youngest champion in 30 years and was among the favorites heading into the 2004 Olympic Trials in New York. Unfortunately, he was slowed by a hamstring strain and finished 23rd at that race in 2:19:20. Ryan joined Team Running USA and trained under legendary coach Joe Vigil, with Olympians such as Meb Keflezighi (2004 Olympic silver medalist) and Deena Kastor (2004 Olympic bronze medalist). Coach Vigil possessed the tough love mentality that Ryan was looking for in a coach and he continued to improve.

Ryan entered the 2008 Olympic Trials in New York as one of the favorites to make the U.S. team. Ryan started well, running with the lead pack at five kilometers, but he never made it to the 10 kilometer mark. He collapsed to the pavement at the five mile mark, was given CPR by bystanders, and taken by an ambulance to Lenox Hill Hospital, where he was pronounced dead. At the tender age of 28, Ryan's life was over. Ryan Shay was a shining star and an outstanding role model. We have such a short time in life and what we do with our life and the people that we impact is important.

Questions for Thought:

1. Ryan Shay lived life to the fullest, not afraid to take challenges. How do you live life to the fullest?

2. We often take life for granted. How do you take advantage of every day?

3. List three things that you will focus on today that will make you appreciate life.

Mel Sheppard

A Weak Heart But Strong Frontrunner

Mel Sheppard had a great influence on the development of middle distance running. Mel was a frontrunner who liked to take the pace out hard. Frontrunners like to challenge the field to keep a fast pace. When a runner takes the race out and leads, other runners can draft behind and save energy. The frontrunner expends a large amount of energy early in the race, which could lead to high levels of fatigue at the end of the race. There is a fine line between going out too hard and paying the price later, and being able to hold everyone else off and being victorious.

In the 800-meter final at the 1908 London Olympics, Mel led the field at the half-way mark, running 53.0 for the first 400 meters. He ran the second 400 meters in 59.4 to take the Olympic gold medal in a new world record of 1:52.4. He also won the 1500-meter run; winning the first running gold medal awarded at the 1908 Olympics and tying the world record.

The following Olympiad at the 1912 Stockholm Games, Mel used the same tactics he always did and took it out hard, attempting to destroy the field. After an opening lap of 52.4, he was overtaken by U.S. teammate Ted Meredith, who set a new world record of 1.51.9.

Mel's ability to push the body to the limit as a frontrunner was remarkable. What made the accomplishments of Mel Sheppard all the more remarkable was that early in his career, he applied for a job with the New York City police force, but was rejected because of a weak heart. Amazingly, his races were characterized by the heart of a front-running champion!

Questions for Thought:

1. How do you show heart?

2. Vince Lombardi once said, "Fatigue makes cowards of us all." How do you overcome fatigue when it tries to make a coward out of you?

3. Mel Sheppard was not afraid to risk failure by courageously running a fast pace and "putting it all on the line." How are you able to "put it on the line" and risk failure in order to succeed?

Frank Shorter

Missing the Roar

Frank Shorter ignited the running boom in the United States in the 1970s with his running accomplishments. Frank started as a long distance track runner, winning the NCAA six mile race for Yale in 1969. He went on to win numerous national titles at 10,000 meters and six miles as well as three miles. At the 1972 Olympics, he set a U.S. record and took fifth place in the 10,000 meters. Although he was a great track runner, Frank Shorter will be best remembered as a marathon runner.

Frank's crowning moment came in 1972 in Munich. Ironically, Frank was born in Munich, and in the Munich Olympics he was involved in one of the most bizarre endings of an Olympic marathon ever. On September 10, 1972, the Olympic Marathon started from the Olympic stadium. As the race wore on, Shorter assumed the lead and gradually began to pull away from the field on the streets of Munich, West Germany. His lead grew so large that television cameras could not capture him and trail runners in the same picture. With approximately 15 minutes left in the 26.2-mile race, Frank figured he was so far ahead that if he didn't get run over by a bus, he was going to win.

As Frank neared the tunnel that led into the Olympic stadium, he imagined the reception he would get as the crowd viewed him entering the Olympic stadium to run one final lap to the finish line to become the Olympic champion. Suddenly, Frank heard a roar go up from the crowd. It was the final day of the track and field meet, and Frank figured someone in the stadium had come up with an outstanding performance. As Frank entered the stadium, it was silent. It was not the roaring crowd that he had expected to anoint him as the Olympic victor.

Frank Shorter had been upstaged by an imposter, who had illegally entered the race near the tunnel and started taking a victory lap, drawing the applause meant for the marathon leader. After he crossed the finish line somebody finally clued Frank in to the imposter. Once it was all sorted out, Frank Shorter had the gold medal with the second fastest Olympic marathon time ever of 2:12:19.

Four years later, in the 1976 Montreal Olympic Games, Frank was approaching the tunnel of the Olympic stadium when he once again heard the roar from inside. It was for the guy finishing ahead of him, Waldemar Cierpinski of East Germany, who won the gold. However, as the years passed, proof of East Germany's illegal doping program for its athletes identified Cierpinski as using illegal performance enhancing drugs. Frank Shorter had run to Olympic glory with gold and silver medals in consecutive Olympic marathons. However, due to the circumstances, he never heard the roar of victory.

Questions for Thought:

1. Do you compete to hear the crowd roar or compete for the inner roar of self-satisfaction?

2. Does someone you know get a lot of the credit you feel you deserve? How do you handle that situation?

3. How do you appreciate the journey to the finish line?

Christian Smith

Diving To the Line

Christian Smith grew up in the small town of Garfield, Kansas, and ran track at tiny Pawnee Heights High School, leading his team to state titles in 2000 and 2002. The summer between his high school junior and senior years, he won the 800 meters at the AAU National Junior Olympics. Christian was awarded a partial scholarship to Kansas State University and his sophomore year, in 2004, he won the Big XII 1000-meter run, setting a school record. He qualified for the U.S. Olympic Trials at 800 meters and placed fifth in his semifinal heat, barely missing the finals by one place.

Christian continued to train and quietly gain confidence while at K-State. He was an indoor NCAA Champion in the mile, the collegiate record holder in the indoor 1000 meters, and he also set the indoor 1000, outdoor 800 and 1500-meter school records. In preparation for the upcoming 2008 Olympic Trials, he moved to Eugene, Oregon, to train with the Oregon Track Club. However, he lost his entire 2007 season when his appendix ruptured and an infection set in. Fighting the illness, he battled to qualify for the Olympic Trials. Only 30 people qualify to run at the trials in the 800 meters and Christian was originally listed as the 31st qualifier, but made the field when a couple of runners dropped out. Most thought he had no chance to make the team.

Christian qualified through the rounds to the 800-meter final. Starting off slowly, Christian gradually worked his way up through the field. As the pack came out of the final turn and into the home stretch at the University of Oregon's Hayward Field, Nick Symmonds moved into the lead, followed by Andrew Wheating. The battle for third place and the final spot on the U.S. Olympic 800-meter team was between Khadevis Robinson, the pre-race favorite, and Christian Smith. Both lunged at the finish, throwing their bodies through the air to try to out lean the other and ended up sprawled on the ground after the race. As Christian lay on the ground, the results flashed on the scoreboard, and by the slimmest of margins, he had made the Olympic team.

It was a 1-2-3 sweep for hometown-trained athletes in what has been called one of the most dramatic races in U.S. Olympic Trials history. The man nobody expected to make the team had kept his focus and faith to persevere and reach his goal.

Questions for Thought:

1. Many people gave up on Christian making the Olympic team, but he continued to believe in himself. Do you have a strong belief in yourself?

2. Christian came from a small high school to eventually run on the world's biggest athletic stage, the Olympics. Does where you come from limit you in being successful?

3. Christian dove across the finish line to make the team. What are you prepared to do when you are in a battle to accomplish your goals?

Tommie Smith

Standing For His Rights

Tommie Smith set many school records in high school and was voted "Most Valuable Athlete" three years straight in basketball, football, and track and field. While a student at San Jose State, he began making a name for himself by winning the NCAA 220-yard title in 1967, as well as adding the AAU 200-meter championship. Tommie was coached by Bud Winter, whose stable of fast sprinters were nicknamed "Speed City" and set several world records in the relays.

In the 1968 200-meter Olympic final in Mexico City, Tommie blazed home in a world record time of 19.83, even though he slowed down as he neared the finish line with his fists held high. Peter Norman of Australia finished second and John Carlos of the U.S. was third. At the awards ceremony, both Tommie and Carlos climbed onto the podium, and as the *Star Spangled Banner* played, they were each wearing one black glove; Tommie's on his right hand, Carlos' on his left. Tommie later stated that his right handed demonstration was meant to represent Black Power in America. The left hand demonstration of Carlos was meant to represent unity in Black America. The black socks that both wore without shoes represented black poverty in America.

At the time of the demonstrations, the actions were considered disrespectful and resulted in both men being expelled from the Olympic village. They were suspended by the United States Olympic Committee and ordered to leave Mexico City immediately. When the two men returned to America, they were greeted as heroes by the African-American community and as unpatriotic troublemakers by others. Both men suffered threats against their lives.

Cheered by some, jeered by others, and ignored by many more, Tommie Smith made a commitment to dedicate his life, even at great personal risk, to champion the cause of oppressed people. Today, his historic achievements make him a nationally and internationally distinguished figure in African American history. Tommie Smith's courageous leadership, talent, and activism have earned him well-deserved athletic and humanitarian awards.

Questions for Thought:

1. Tommie had the courage to stand up for what he thought was right. Do you have the courage to stand up for what you believe in?

2. Tommie was expelled from the Olympic Village. What sacrifices might you have to make to stand up for what you believe in?

3. Tommie is now viewed as a hero. What are the characteristics of a hero?

Dwight Stones

The One That Got Away

Dwight Stones was one of the world's top high jumpers from 1972 to 1984. He was just 18 years old when he represented the U.S. for the first time at the 1972 Olympic Games, placing third in the high jump competition. The following year in 1973 in Munich, Germany, he set his first world record when he cleared 7-6½. That jump also made him the first "flop" jumper to set a world high jump record, five years after Dick Fosbury made the jumping style famous while winning the Mexico City Olympics.

Dwight was considered an overwhelming favorite for the 1976 Olympic title in Montreal. He had won the NCAA Indoor and Outdoor Championships that year while at Long Beach State. The day of the Olympic high jump final, it began to rain and Dwight's form and confidence began to fall apart. He had to settle for a bronze medal. Just four days after the 1976 Olympics high jump, Stones demonstrated he was the best jumper in the world by setting his final world record of 7-7¼.

Dwight was one of the top high jumpers in the world, but was unable to win an Olympic gold mdeal. In 1980, the U.S. boycotted the Moscow Games and Dwight would lose yet another opportunity to win Olympic Gold.

Dwight missed the 1979 season after being suspended for receiving money in a Superstars competition, but made a comeback to prepare for the 1984 Olympics in his home state of California. To qualify for the Olympics, Dwight won the U.S. Trials, setting his 13th American record in the high jump. However, in the Olympic Games in Los Angeles, he would again fail to win Olympic gold, placing fourth. Dwight later went on to successfully cover track and field as a television personality.

In his 16-year career, he won an incredible 19 national championships with more No. 1 world rankings than any other high jumper in history, but he failed to win the big one.

Questions for Thought:

1. Dwight was successful for a long period of time. Think of something you were successful in early on in life and have continued to improve in.

2. Dwight lost an opportunity when the U.S. boycotted the 1980 Olympic Games. How do you handle lost opportunities?

3. Dwight now contributes to the sport of track and field as an announcer. What will you give back to the sport when your competitive days are over?

John Taylor

First African-American to Win a Gold Medal

John Taylor was born in Washington, D.C. and then moved to Philadelphia. In high school, he became the best prep quarter-miler in the nation running the 440 yards in 50.6. At the time, there were few African Americans as role models in track and field and none as talented as John. He attended the University of Pennsylvania, where he was the only African American on the team. In 1907, he had established himself as the top quarter-miler in the world, setting the world record of 48.6.

John's race strategy was to allow his opponents to run ahead of him, and then chase them down from behind in the homestretch. It was this strategy that made him such an effective anchor on the relay teams he competed on. That same strategy allowed him to make up 20 yards during the Olympic Trials, where he won the 400-meter race in 49.8.

In the 1908 London Olympics, John had opportunities in both the open 400-meter race and the 4x400-meter relay teams. Controversy erupted in the 400-meter race. Leading up to the Olympics, John had not been as dominant in the 400 meters as he had the previous years, and Englishman Wyndham Halswelle was considered to be the favorite. John's U.S. teammate, John Carpenter, ran a surprising race and was passing Halswelle on the final stretch to take the lead when British officials determined that he cut off Halswelle. Because of the foul, officials stopped the race immediately, not allowing the runners to finish. John was 20 meters back at the time, but some experts felt he would have unleashed his famous kick to win the race. However, John indicated he wasn't feeling well, ill from a respiratory infection he had picked up in London.

The disputed foul led to a decision to re-run the 400-meter race the next day. The Americans disputed the call and displayed a show of solidarity for their disqualified American teammate, John Carpenter. Both John and the other American, William Robbins refused to compete in the race.

John Taylor made history when he became the first African American to win a gold medal, running on the 4x400-meter relay team that set a world record. After returning home to Philadelphia, Taylor never recovered from the respiratory distress that began in the damp conditions of England. He developed typhoid pneumonia and at the age of 26, he died; a mere four months after winning Olympic gold.

Questions for Thought:

1. John Taylor was one of the first great African American role models in track and field. Who are some of your role models?

2. How do you become an effective role model?

3. John Taylor died only four months after winning a gold medal. What are some things you should appreciate that you may take for granted?

Jim Thorpe

The World's Greatest Athlete

James Francis Thorpe was born in a one-room cabin near Prague, Oklahoma. He was a descendant of the last great Sauk and Fox chief, Black Hawk; a noted warrior and athlete. Jim and his twin brother, Charlie, attended the Sac and Fox Indian Agency School together until Charlie died from pneumonia at the age of 9. Jim did not like school and ran away several times, so his father sent him to Haskell Institute, an Indian boarding school in Lawrence, Kansas. His mother died during his youth, and in 1904, Jim decided to attend Carlisle Industrial Indian School in Pennsylvania. Later that year, his father died and Jim again dropped out of school to farm before later returning to Carlisle. At Carlisle, Jim started his athletic career playing football and running track. He was a three-time All-American football player, leading Carlisle to the National Collegiate Championship.

He was also a remarkable track athlete. At the 1912 Olympics, two new multi-event disciplines were included, the pentathlon and the decathlon. The pentathlon consisted of the long jump, javelin throw, 200-meter dash, discus and the 1500-meter run. At the Stockholm, Sweden, Olympics Jim was a busy man, competing in the pentathlon, decathlon, long jump, and high jump. He convincingly won both multi-events, setting Olympic records. His decathlon record would stand for nearly two decades. He placed fourth in the high jump and seventh in the long jump. His performances were all the more remarkable because someone had stolen his shoes just before he was due to compete. He found two different sized shoes and wore extra socks because one shoe was too big.

In 1913, Jim's wins were jeopardized when officials realized he had played two semiprofessional seasons of baseball. At that time, the Olympic Committee had strict rules about Olympians receiving money for participating in professional athletics. His name was removed from the record books and his gold medals were taken away. In 1984, 30 years after his death, the International Olympic Committee finally restored his Olympic medals.

Questions for Thought:

1. Jim was not focused as a student early in his life, but learned to focus when he competed to be successful. How do you go about achieving focus?

2. Jim was always willing to try new challenges. How will your level of success be defined by your willingness to take on challenges?

3. Jim did not receive his proper accolades for his accomplishments until after he had died. How important is it to properly honor achievements?

Lasse Virén

Down But Not Out

Lasse Virén added to the legend of great Finnish distance runners when he won the 5000 and 10,000-meter events at two consecutive Olympics in 1972 and 1976. Lasse debuted on the international track and field scene in 1971 and entered the 1972 Olympic Games in Munich as an underdog. In the 10,000-meter final, Lasse ran with the pack until the 12th of 26 laps and then his feet became tangled with Emiel Puttemans of Belgium. Lasse fell hard to the track, as did Tunisia's Mohamed Gammoudi. Lasse got up as quickly as he could, but he had lost 30 meters to the lead field. His Olympic dream was quickly slipping away.

Falling in any race puts a runner at a distinct disadvantage. Falling in the Olympic Games when one must run at his best is almost impossible to recover from. The pace is thrown off and physically the fall may affect a runner's running mechanics. Adrenaline takes over and runners tend to overcompensate and try to gain ground back too fast, leading to heavy fatigue at the end of the race. With 600 meters to go in the race, Lasse was feeling the fatigue from having used the extra energy to catch the pack. Facing a decision to drop back or go for the win, with tremendous courage and determination, he made his move and started an unprecedented lap and a half kick that only Puttemans was able to respond to. Puttemans could not match the Finn's kick and Lasse won, breaking the world record in a time of 27:28.40.

A week later, Lasse ran the 5000 meters final and after a tactical first two miles, the pace quickened over the final mile. Lasse matched the move of Steve Prefontaine, sprinted past Gammoudi with 120 meters to go, and won in 13:26.4. Four days later, despite the wet, chilly, and windy weather in Helsinki, Finland, he set a new world record at 5000 meters by running 13:16.4

At the 1976 Summer Olympics in Montreal, Lasse again won both events to make it a "double double", becoming the only repeat winner of the 5000-meter race in Olympic history. Eighteen hours after the 5000-meter final, he competed in the men's marathon and finished fifth in 2:13:11.

He returned to compete at the 1980 Olympics and finished fifth in the 10,000, the only event he competed in. He had no other major successes other than at the Olympics, and was considered a master of being able to manage his training to peak at the absolute perfect moment. His gold medal and world record in 10,000 meters will always be remembered, as he fell, quickly caught up, and courageously ran away from the field.

Questions for Thought:

1. Have you had things go against you and you stayed down for a while? How did that make you feel?

2. Have you been knocked down, but quickly got back up to pursue your goals? How did you do it?

3. If you see your goal slipping away, how do you react?

Cornelius "Dutch" Warmerdam

The Flying Dutchman

Cornelius "Dutch" Warmerdam began pole vaulting by practicing in his father's peach and apricot orchard with a bamboo pole. He developed into one of the most dominant athletes of the 1940s. Before 1940, many experts thought it was impossible for humans to vault 15-0. Today's pole vaulters use fiberglass poles and land in soft cushioned mats; however, in the 1940s, pole vaulters used rigid bamboo poles and landed in sand and sawdust pits.

Dutch went to college at Fresno State University and started winning National Amateur Athletic Union titles while inching towards the magic 15 foot barrier. Dutch attended a small meet in Berkeley, California, and flew over the bar set at 15-0. An "unbreakable" barrier had been achieved! He eventually raised the world record to 15-7¾, a record that would stand an incredible 15 years. He also set the world indoor record at 15-8½ and made 43 vaults over the once impossible height of 15 feet.

Despite being the most dominant United States pole vaulter ever, Dutch never got to compete in the Olympic Games, as he had the misfortune to be at his peak during World War II and the canceled Olympic Games of 1940 and 1944. With bamboo in short supply after the war, pole vaulting changed dramatically. Metal poles replaced bamboo and they were soon replaced with fiberglass.

In 1947, Dutch started coaching and although he was still the best pole vaulter in the world when the 1948 Olympics came, he was not eligible to participate in the Olympic Games because making money by coaching disqualified him from amateur competition. Dutch went on to a successful 20-year head coaching career at Fresno State University.

Questions for Thought:

1. Dutch used a bamboo pole and landed in sand or sawdust pits. How can equipment help you perform?

2. Dutch missed two Olympics Games because of a war that he had no control over. What things do you worry about that you have no control over?

3. What are the major things that you can control that will make you successful?

Mal Whitfield

Marvelous Mal

Mal Whitfield's father died when Mal was 4-years-old. At 12, his mother died and he barely avoided being sent to an orphanage. His sister, Betty Clark, obtained a court order to gain custody. After his high school graduation in 1943, he joined the Army Air Force and later attended Ohio State University. He won the NCAA title in the 800 meters in 1948 and 880-yard run in 1949.

As a 23-year-old, Mal won both the 400 meters and 800 meters in the U.S. Olympic Trials to qualify for the 1948 London Olympic Games. Mal, a master tactical runner, stayed cool and poised early in the 800-meter race, then attacked on the backstretch, taking the lead to win in an Olympic record of 1:49.2. Mal won two more medals at the London Games, picking up a bronze in the 400 meters and running a leg on the victorious U.S. 4x400-meter relay team. Including the preliminary heats and finals, Mal ran nine races in eight days and became the first U.S. military serviceman on active duty to win a gold medal in the Olympics.

Between the 1948 and 1952 Olympics, Mal completed his military service, which included 27 combat missions as an aerial gunner during the Korean War. In between bombing missions over North Korea, he trained at night on the runways. The improvised training paid off as Mal set a world record in the 880 yard run of 1:49.2 in 1950, running on a slow track due to heavy rains. Later, Mal beat Wes Santee to lower the world record to 1:48.6.

The 1952 Olympics in Helsinki, Finland, featured basically the same runners in the 800-meter field as the previous Olympics. Mal, again, made the strong move down the backstretch to open up the lead and repeat his 800-meter victory. He also earned a silver medal as a member of the U.S. 4x400-meter relay team. His long rhythmical strides, ability to run relaxed, and skill to quickly change paces allowed him to reign as the dominant force in the 800 meters. From 1946 to 1955, Mal won 66 of 69 major middle distance races throughout the world.

Mal Whitfield went on to work for the U.S. State Department, conducting sports clinics in Africa. In his 47 years in Africa, he played a key role in training and developing African athletes who represented their countries as Olympians, and he arranged athletic scholarships for over 5000 African athletes to study in the United States.

Questions for Thought:

1. Mal improvised his training during the war. What conditions might cause you to improvise your training program?

2. Mal was a great tactical runner. What is your best tactic? What tactics could you improve on? How will you improve on those tactics?

3. Mal ran nine races in eight days at the Olympics. How do you prepare yourself mentally and physically to compete in multiple events?

Rick Wohlhuter

Get Up and Going

Rick Wohlhuter was a two-time Olympian and qualified for the Olympic Games in both the 800 and 1500-meter events. Rick launched his successful career with two high school state championships in Illinois. At the 1972 Olympic Trials, Rick placed second to Dave Wottle in the 800 meters. Rick seemed to be a certain Olympic finalist and possible medalist. Dave Wottle won the Olympic Games 800 meters, but Rick's Olympic dream ended quite differently. Running in the 800 meters semifinal, he was tripped, fell to the ground, and was unable to qualify for the final. Rick was tremendously disappointed, as he was ready to race well and contend for a medal. However, he didn't stay down for long.

In the years between Olympics, Rick got up and got going again at a strong, fast, record shattering pace, breaking the world record for the half mile twice. He was a master at race tactics and preferred a fast pace through the first 400 or 600 meters so he could run fast times. Rick was a study in tenacity and aggression; his strength and speed enabled him to qualify for both the 800 and 1500 meters at the 1976 Montreal Olympics.

The Montreal 800-meter final included an outstanding field, but Rick was determined to make up for his fall in the previous Olympic Games. Rick ran a masterful race, giving everything he had to capture the bronze medal in 1:44.12. It took a world record by Alberto Juantorena in 1:43.50 to beat him! Rick also went on to place sixth in the 1500 meters in 3:40.64. Rick retired in 1977.

Questions for Thought:

1. Rick Wohluter fell down in the Olympics Games but used the experience for motivation for a future Olympic medal. Have you fallen at some task and remained down?

2. What does it take to get up and get going again?

3. Rick was a master at running tactics. Do you study and prepare to be a master at the events you participate in?

John Woodruff

Long John

John Woodruff grew up with a brother and eight sisters in Connellsville, Pennsylvania, as the grandson of Virginia slaves. Football was his favorite sport until he had to quit because it didn't give him enough time to do his chores. John eventually had to quit school to find employment during the Great Depression, but he found it hard for a black man to find work, so he returned to school and began his track career. A tall and gangly runner, John had an unorthodox running style but a long stride length.

John set the Pennsylvania state high school half-mile and mile records as well as the national mile record. As a freshman at the University of Pittsburg he won the 1936 Olympic Trials 800 meters, qualifying him to the 1936 Olympics in Berlin. The 1936 Olympics were shrouded in controversy when Adolf Hitler attempted to use the Olympics to demonstrate his Aryan supremacy theory. Many Americans considered a boycott; however, American black track stars felt the U.S. should attempt to improve conditions in America before improving conditions in Germany.

In Berlin, John made it through the qualifying heats of the 800-meter run to make the final. The 21-year-old freshman with no international experience found himself in a predicament in the final. With 300 meters to go, he appeared to be hopelessly boxed in along the rail. John had no option except to stop. As he stopped, the runners passed him by, and then John moved into lane three and started running again. He was now in last place, but his long powerful strides made up the ground. His superiority over the field allowed him to not only overcome the tremendous mistake and catch the field, but also to pass them and capture the win in 1:52.9

John was one of 10 black athletes who won a combined total of 14 medals at the Games and embarrassed Hitler's white supremacy theory. Back home, John was a hero. He had an outstanding career, which might have been much greater, but World War II canceled the next two Olympics. In his last race, in 1940, he set an American record of 1:48.6 that lasted 12 years.

Questions for Thought:

1. John Woodruff is a forgotten hero. How can you best honor those who came before you and set the stage for your success?

2. John was born with natural ability and used it to achieve success. What are you doing with your natural ability?

3. John's Olympic chances appeared hopeless when he got boxed in, but his fighting spirit came through. How would you rate your fighting spirit on a scale of 1-10?

Dave Wottle

From Out of Nowhere

During his childhood, Dave Wottle was so thin and weak that the family doctor told him that he needed to take up running to strengthen himself. That was the start of Dave's running career. Dave attended Bowling Green University and within one week, brought his personal best time for 880 yards down from 1:51.6 to 1:47.8. He placed second in the mile at the 1970 NCAA Outdoor Championships. He was hampered by injuries and missed the entire 1971 season; however, he came back in 1972 and won the 1500 meters at the NCAA Outdoor Track and Field Championships. At the 1973 NCAA Outdoor Track and Field Championships, he won the mile run in a time of 3:57.1, an NCAA record.

Leading up to the 1972 Olympic Games in Munich, Germany, he surprisingly won and equaled the 800-meter world record of 1:44.3 at the U.S. Olympic Trials. In the Olympic 800-meter final, Dave lined up at the start wearing his familiar golf cap. From the gun, the pace was fast and Dave immediately dropped to the rear of the field, running last in the eight-man field for the first 500 meters. Down the backstretch, he started to move up and began passing runner after runner in the final straight away, finally passing the leader in the final meter, barely winning by just 0.03. In a world class 800-meter race, the runners usually run faster at the beginning and then slow down as fatigue begins to set in. Dave (nicknamed Wottle the Throttle) ran an even-paced race with each 200 meter split in 26.0.

At the victory ceremony, Dave forgot to remove his golf cap during the playing of the national anthem. Some people interpreted this as a form of protest, but he later apologized and explained that he simply forgot to take it off during the emotional ceremony. He originally wore his signature cap to keep his hair out of his face. After realizing the cap was part of his identity, he wore it for the remainder of his career.

Questions for Thought:

1. Have you been in a situation where you got behind early and were tempted to give up? What did you do?

2. What should you focus on when you are getting beat?

3. Think of a situation where you performed well when you least expected it.

Kevin Young

Walk-on to World Record

Kevin Young was born and raised in the Watts section of Southern California. His upbringing in the inner city during a time when gang warfare was on the rise gave him many opportunities to fall in with the wrong crowd, but the support of his family helped him avoid the wrong path. In high school track and field, Kevin first focused on the jumping events, but then turned to the hurdles as a sophomore. His senior year, he finished third in the 110-meter high hurdles at the California State Championships and had a personal record of 37.54 in the 300-meter intermediate hurdles. Despite his high school success, it was not enough to earn him a scholarship offer to a major university, so Kevin walked on at UCLA.

Kevin entered his freshman year as a skinny, 6-4, 18-year-old, thinking his best event was the 110-meter high hurdles. However, his coach envisioned his potential to develop into an Olympic caliber 400-meter hurdler. By his junior year, Kevin won the NCAA Championships in the 400-meter hurdles and repeated the following year in a meet record time of 47.85. He also ran on the UCLA 4x400-meter relay team that became the first collegiate relay team to break 3:00, blazing to a 2:59.91 at the 1987 NCAA Championships. Kevin, the walk-on, ran the fastest split.

At the 1988 U.S. Olympic Trials, Kevin finished third to make the U.S. team to compete in the Olympic Games in South Korea. Kevin finished fourth and laid the groundwork that would lead to future greatness. In his preparation for the 1992 Olympic Games, Kevin decided that he would have to do something different with his stride pattern. Working with Coach John Smith, they came up with a pattern of taking only 12 steps between hurdles four and five. Based on the times he had been running in practice, he believed he was capable of running under 47 seconds. He wrote his goal time of 46.89 on the walls of his room and on his shoes.

At the 1992 Olympics in Barcelona, Spain, Kevin executed his strategy to perfection, clearing the first hurdle in 19 strides, hurdles two and three in 13, hurdles four and five in 12, and 13 the rest of the way. He slammed the 10th barrier with the heel of his lead leg, but it didn't matter. He was already several meters ahead of his nearest opponent. Five meters from the finish line, he threw a fist in the air before crossing the line in a new Olympic and world record time of 46.78, more than a full tenth of a second faster than his own goal of 46.89. Kevin did what many believed to be impossible. He broke the 400-meter hurdle world record of 47.02 set by the great Edwin Moses and became the first man to break the 47.0 barrier in that event.

Questions for Thought:

1. Kevin was a walk-on at UCLA. Are you willing to make a commitment without any financial benefits?

2. Despite already being successful, Kevin wasn't afraid to get out of his comfort zone and try new things. Are you willing to try new things to improve?

3. Kevin set a high goal and went for it. What determines how high you set your goal?

Louis Zamperini

Devil at His Heels

Louis Zamperini was a juvenile troublemaker that had a knack for getting into trouble, so his brother got him to go out for high school track. Louie ran the mile in 4:21.2 and set a new national high school record. He went to the University of Southern California and competed in the U.S. Olympic Trials in 1936. Louie finished second in the 5000 meters at the trials to qualify for the Olympics to be held in Berlin, Germany. He finished eighth in the Olympic 5000-meter final, running the last lap in a blazing 56 seconds, catching the attention of Adolf Hitler. Upon returning to college in 1938, Louie set a national collegiate mile record, which stood for 15 years. He was also a part of many national record breaking relay teams. He may have broken the four-minute mile had he not joined the United States Army Air Force as a bombardier in the South Pacific during World War II.

Louie was deployed to Hawaii, and after flying a number of missions his aircraft was shot down. Louie and two other soldiers lived through the crash in the Pacific Ocean. The soldiers had hope that search planes would rescue them. Fighting storms, sharks, lack of drinking water and food, as well as enemy attacks, the soldiers drifted day after day on a small raft. After 47 days adrift in the ocean, the Japanese Navy rescued Louie and the only other surviving soldier. The Japanese held Louie in captivity in a brutal prisoner camp. One particular guard wanted to make an example of the eternally optimistic Olympic runner, and for two years the guard tried to break Louie's spirit with verbal and physical cruelty. He faced daily beatings, inhumane treatment, and lack of food. His weight dropped from 160 pounds before the plane crash to 67 pounds. The threat of mass execution was constant for two and a half years until the end of the war. He was listed as killed in action and his family feared he was dead. Despite all the difficulties, Louie focused on keeping his mind sharp and maintaining a positive spirit.

After the war was over, Louie returned to a hero's welcome but that did not last long. He had hopes of coming back to run in the Olympics again, but war injuries would not allow him to train. He constantly had bad nightmares and turned to alcohol.

His life changed when he met evangelist Billy Graham, who helped him launch a new career as a Christian inspirational speaker. One of his favorite themes was "forgiveness," and he visited many of the guards from his prison camp days to let them know that he had forgiven them.

Questions for Thought:

1. Louis Zamperini spent 47 days on a raft without food and water, but kept up his positive attitude. What can you learn from this story?

2. Often times, we think we have it tough. Does Louie's story make you believe you have it easy? How could you toughen up?

3. Louie forgave the guards that committed some of the worst war crimes in history. How do you rate your ability to forgive on a scale of 1-10 (10 high)?

Emil Zátopek

The Czech Locomotive

Emil Zátopek was born in Koprivnice, Czechoslovakia, as the sixth child of a modest family. At age 16, Emil left home to work at the Bata shoe factory. When Bata sponsored a race, he was persuaded to enter. Out of the field of 100, Emil finished second and he began to take a serious interest in the sport.

Lacking natural talent, Emil relied on determination. He worked by day and ran by night in heavy boots in mounds of snow with a flashlight in hand. He had no coach, so he created his own workouts by studying the great Paavo Nurmi of Finland. Coaches laughed at Emil's training routine, but eventually, his methods became the norm. When the Nazis occupied Czechoslovakia during World War II, Emil continued to practice under German supervision inside sport stadiums. Still, the war cost Emil his prime.

The 5-8, 145 pound athlete made his Olympic debut in 1948 at the age of 26, where he won gold in the 10,000 meters and missed the 5000 meters gold by one meter. Two months prior to the 1952 Olympic Games in London, doctors ordered Emil not to compete due to a gland infection. He ignored their advice and won gold medals and set Olympic records in the 5000 and 10,000-meter races. The same afternoon as his 5000-meter win, his wife Dana won gold in the javelin. He later called it the most rewarding day of his career. However, Emil wasn't satisfied. He decided to test his limits in the marathon.

Since he knew nothing about marathon strategy, he planned to shadow world record holder Jim Peters of Great Britain. The first 15 kilometers, Emil raced beside Peters. Peters knew the pace was fast and he had gone out too hard when Emil asked the Englishman what he thought of the race thus far. The astonished Peters told the Czech that the pace was "too slow," in an attempt to fool him, at which point Emil simply accelerated away to win in Olympic record time. Emil attempted to defend his marathon gold medal in 1956, but was hospitalized for six weeks after he suffered a groin injury and never regained his form, finishing sixth. He retired from competition in 1957.

His running style was distinctive and very much at odds with what was considered to be an efficient style at the time. His head would often roll, face contorted with effort, while his torso swung from side to side. He often wheezed and panted audibly while running, which earned him the nicknames of "Emil the Terrible" or "the Czech Locomotive". Emil Zátopek is credited with changing running and training by developing intense interval workouts that have become the standard of modern training methods.

Questions for Thought:

1. Emil Zátopek is credited with interval training. He would do as many as 40x400 meters. What's the hardest workout you have ever done?

2. No matter what the weather, Emil would train outdoors. What keeps you from training consistently? How could you remove those barriers?

3. Emil went out of his comfort zone to step up to the challenge and win an Olympic gold in his first marathon. List three challenges that would take you out of your comfort zone.

Jan Železný

Mighty Thrower

The first sport for Jan Železný from Czechoslovakia was handball, but with two parents that threw the javelin, it was only a matter of time before he would become a javelin thrower. Jan entered the 1988 Olympics in Seoul, South Korea, as the world record holder in the javelin throw. He started off well, setting an Olympic record in the qualifying round and leading the competition until the last thrower of the last round, Tapio Korjus of Finland, out threw him by six inches. Losing the competition on the last throw provided Jan the motivation to continue to improve.

Jan's goal was to establish himself as the best javelin thrower in the world. However, he failed to qualify for the final in either the 1990 European Championships or the 1991 World Championships. But Jan was determined to be a big meet thrower and focused on rising to meet the challenge. Jan qualified for the 1992 Barcelona Olympics, eager to improve upon his previous Olympics. In his first throw of the final, he broke his own Olympic record by over 12-0, with a throw of 294-2, which held up to win the gold medal.

Jan reached the summit of success a few months before the 1996 Olympics, when he pushed the world record out to an amazing 323-1. At 170 pounds, he was the lightest of the javelin competitors entered in the 1996 Atlanta Olympics. Steve Backley of Great Britain took the early lead in the first round, but Jan passed him in the second round with a throw that was good enough to win his second gold medal.

Jan's career was threatened in 1998 when he was forced to undergo shoulder surgery, but a rigorous rehabilitation program allowed him to come back to win the bronze medal at the 1999 World Championships in Seville, Spain.

Jan was again the lightest javelin competitor in the 2000 Sydney, Australia Olympics, but captured his third Olympic gold medal and set an Olympic record of 295-10. At 38 years of age, Jan competed in his final Olympic Games in 2004 in Athens, finishing in ninth place. Jan's motto of "work and sacrifice" served him well during his career as the greatest javelin thrower ever.

Questions for Thought:

1. What does the motto "work and sacrifice" mean to you?

2. Jan was the smallest competitor in two Olympics and won the competition. What are the important factors that go into being successful?

3. Jan was a big meet thrower. What type of attitude do "big meet performers" have going into major competitions?

References

Abebe Bikila. (n.d.). Retrieved from www.ethiopians.com/abebe_bikila.htm.

Adelson, E. (2004, August 9). *Ray Ewry wasn't even supposed to walk.* Retrieved September 10, 2010 from http://sports.espn.go.com/oly/summer04/trackandfield/columns/story?id=1862509

Alden, R. (1956, November 26). This Day in Sports: Parson Bob Vaults to a Second Gold. *The New York Times.* Retrieved from http://www.nytimes.com/packages/html/sports/year_in_sports/11.26.html

Al Joyner (n.d.) http://www.aljoyner.com/

Athletics Australia. (n.d.). *Ron Clarke MBE.* Retrieved November 21, 2010, from http://www.athletics.com.au/fanzone/hall_of_fame/ron_clarke

Austin, C. (2007). *Head Games, Life's Greatest Challenges.* Austin, TX: Turnkey Press.

Baker, W. (2012). Profiles: Horace Ashenfelter. *Running Past.* Retrieved from http://www.runningpast.com/horace_ashenfelter.htm

Bannister, R. (1981). *The Four Minute Mile.* New York, NY: Lyons and Burford.

Bascomb, N. (2004). The Perfect Mile: *Three Athletes, One Goal, and Less Than Four Minutes to Achieve It.* New York, NY: Houghton- Mifflin.

Bass, A. (2002). *Not TheTriumph But The Struggle*. Minneapolis, MN: University of Minnesota Press.

Beamon, B. & Beamon, M.W. (1999). *The Man Who Could Fly: The Bob Beamon Story*. Columbus, MS: Genesis Press.

Benyo, R., Henderson, J. (2001). *Running Encyclopedia: The Ultimate Source for Todays Runner.* Champaign, IL: Human Kinetics.

Bishop, G. (2005, November 27). The longest run: The story of Gerry Lindgren. *The Seattle Times.* Retrieved from http://seattletimes.nwsource.com/html/sports/2002648977_lindgren27.html

Bloom, M. (1997). *Steve Scott the Miler.* New York, NY: Macmillan.

Bloom, M. (2001). *Run with the Champions.* New York, NY: Rodale Press.

Bob Schul Web Site. (n.d.) http://www.bobschul.net/

Brant, J. (2004). *Duel in the Sun: The Story of Alberto Salazar, Dick Beardsley, and America's Greatest Marathon.* New York, NY: Rodale Press.

Buford, K., *Native American Son, The Life and Sporting Legend of Jim Thorpe*. Lincoln, NE: University of Nebraska -Bison Books

Butcher, P. (2004). *The Perfect Distance - Ovett and Coe*. London, England: Weidenfeld & Nicolson.

Charles Austin: Olympic Gold Medalist & Fitness Expert. (2008). Retrieved October 20, 2010 from http://charlesaustin.net/index.html

Coe, S. (2012). *Running My Life- the Autobiography*. Hatchette, United Kingdom: Hodder

Cunningham, G. & Sand G. (1981). *Never Quit*. Lincoln, VA: Chosen Books Publishing.

Ellick, A. (2001, March). Emil Zatopek. *Running Times*. Retrieved October 17, 2010 from http://runningtimes.Article.aspx?ArticleID=5518

Fitzpatrick,F. (2004, August 19). Immortality wasn't in his plan 1896 Olympic hero Robert Garrett was just looking for fun. *The Inquirer*. Retrieved from http://articles.philly.com/2004-08-19/sports/25392601_1_olympic-discus-baron-pierre-greek-competitor

Finch, P. (1977). *Decathlon Challenge - Bruce Jenner's Story*. Upper Saddle River, NJ: Prentice Hall.

Finder, C. (2006, August 4). 70 years ago today, Connellsville native John Woodruff sprinted from last to first to win gold at Berlin Olympics. *Pittsburg Post Gazette*. Retrieved December 10, 2012 from http://www.post-gazette.com/stories/sports/more-sports/70-years-ago-today-connellsville-native-john-woodruff-sprinted-from-last-to-first-to-win-gold-at-berlin-olympics-444899/

Flatter, R. (2000, December 20). *Three-peating wasn't enough for Oerter*. Retrieved November 1, 2010 from http://espn.go.com/sportscentury/features/00016388.html

Friend, T. (n.d.). Dream Chaser. *ESPN Outside the Lines*. Retrieved from http://sports.espn.go.com/espn/eticket/story?page=090826/flojo

Gotaas, T. Graves, P. (2012). Running A Global History. Reaktion Books.

Hendershott, J. (2008, October). The Biggest Surprise of All? *Track and Field News*, 60-61.

Hildebrand, L. *Unbroken*. (2010). New York, NY: Random House.

Halberg, M. & Gilmour, G. (1963). *A Clean Pair of Heels: The Murray Halberg Story*. London: A.H. & A.W. Reed.

Hoffer, R. (2009). *Something in the Air: American Passion and Defiance in the 1968 Mexico City Olympics*. New York, NY: Simon & Schuster.

Hollobaugh, J. (2012). *The 100 Greatest Track and Field Battles of the 20th Century*. CreateSpace.

Huth, J. (2006, July 9). Remember when? Bob Richards' Olympic Gold Medals. *Illinihq.com*. Retrieved November 28, 2012 from http://www.illinihq.com/sports/illini-sports/track/2006-07-09/remember-when-bob-richards-olympic-gold-medals.html

Hymans, R. (2004). *The History of the U. S. Olympic Trials - Track & Field 1908-2000*. Indianapolis, IN: USA Track and Field.

Ingrady, D. (2011, January 27). College Champion, Fledgling Pro. *The New York Times*. Retrieved January 29, 2011 from http://www.nytimes.com/2011/01/28/sports/28track.html

International Association of Athletics Federation. (n.d.). http://www.iaaf.org/athletes

International Association of Athletics Federation. (2006, May 23). *King of Middle Distance, Hicham El Guerrouj retires.*Retrieved October 28, 2010, from http://www.iaaf.org/news/Kind=2/newsId=34753.html

Jim Thorpe The World's Greatest Athlete (n.d.). http://www.cmgww.com/sports/thorpe/bio/bio.html

Johnson, D. (n.d.). John Baxter Taylor. *Ivy League Black History*. Retrieved December 1, 2012 from http://ivy50.com/blackHistory/story.aspx?sid=12/27/2006%2012:00:00%20AM

Johnson, M. (1997). *Slaying the Dragon: How to Turn Your Small Steps to Great Feats*. New York, NY: Harper Collins.

Jordan, T. (1997). *Pre: The Story of America's Greatest Running Legend, Steve Prefontaine*. New York, NY: Rodale Press.

Kansas Historical Society. (2011, February). *Glenn Cunningham*. Retrieved October 22, 2010 from www.kshs.org/kansapedia/glenn-cunningham/12027

Kiell, P. (2006). *American Miler: The Life and Times of Glenn Cunningham*. Halcottsville, NY: Breakaway Books.

Kiliper, S., & Jenner, B. (1980). *The Olympics and Me*. New York, NY: Doubleday.

Lawson, G. (1996). *World Record Breakers in Track and Field Athletics*. Champaign, IL: Human Kinetics.

Layden, T. (2008, June 30). Divide and Conquer. *Sports Illustrated*. Received from http://sportsillustrated.cnn.com/vault/article/magazine/MAG1141115/index.htm

Litsky, F. (2007, November 1) John Woodruff, an Olympian, Dies at 92. *New York Times*. Retrieved from http://www.nytimes.com/2007/11/01/sports/othersports/01woodruff.html?_r=0

Grand Forks Herald. (2004, September 29). *Letter to the Youth of Grand Forks*. Retrieved July 10, 2010 from http://www.pownetwork.org/bios/c/cushman_cliff.pdf

Gotaas, T. Graves, P. (2012) *Running: A Global History*. United Kingdom: Reaktion Books.

Looney, D. (1978, February 13). A Mite Over the Bar. *SI Vault.* Retrieved October 3, 2010 from http://sportsillustrated.cnn.com/vault/article/magazine/MAG1093326/index.htm

Magill, F. (1987). *Great Lives from History*. New York, NY: Salem Press.

Mallon, B., Buchanan, I., & Tishman, J. (1984). *Quest for Gold; The Encyclopedia of American Olympians.* New York, NY: Leisure Press.

Maraniss, D. (2008). *Rome 1960: The Olympics That Changed the World*. New York, NY: Simon & Schuster.

Marin, D. & Gynn, D. (2000). *The Olympic Marathon.* Champaign, IL: Human Kinetics.

Lewis, C., Marx, J. (1992). *Inside Track, My Professional Life in Amateur Track and Field*. New York, NY: Simon and Schuster.

McCasland, D. (2001). *Eric Liddell - Pure Gold.* Grand Rapids, MI: Discovery House.

Mills, B. (1999). *Wokini: A Lakota Journey to Happiness and Self-Understanding*. Carlsbad, CA: Hay House.

Mendes, R. & Mathias, R. (2001). *The Bob Mathias Story.* Sports Publishing LLC.

Moore, K. (2006). *Bowerman and the Men of Oregon: The Story of Oregon's Legendary Coach and Nike's Cofounder.* New York, NY: Rodale Press.

Nash, K. (2009, May 9). The Forgotten Olympian: The Story of John Taylor. *Bleacher Report.* Retrieved December 1, 2012 by http://bleacherreport.com/articles/171264-the-forgotten-olympian-the-story-of-john-taylor

Nelson, C. (1986). *Track's Greatest Champions*. Los Altos, CA: Tafnews Press.

New Zealand Olympic Committee. (n.d.). *Murray Halberg.* Retrieved November 5, 2010, from http://www.zeus-sport.com/Olympic/Athletes/AthleteProfile.aspx?Print=&ContactID=930

O'Brien, D., Botkin, B. (2012) *Clearing Hurdles: The Quest to Be The World's Greatest Athlete.* Indianapolis, IN: Blue River Press.

Official Website of the University of Kansas Athletics Department. (n.d.). *Kansas Relays History.* Retrieved November 15, 2010 from http://www.kuathletics.com/sports/c-relay/spec-rel/relay-history.html

Quercetani, R.L. (2000). *Athletics - A History of Modern Track and Field Athletics (1860-2000) Men and Women.* Milan, Italy: SEP Editricesrl.

Quercetani, R.L. (2002). *Athletics - A World History of Long Distance Running (1880-2002) Men and Women.* Milan, Italy: SEP Editricesrl.

Quercetani, R.L. & Kok, N. (1990). *Athletics- A History of Modern Track and Field Athletics (1860-2000) Men and Women.* Milan, Italy: Vallardi & Associates.

Penn Biographies: John Baxter Taylor. (n.d.). University Archives and Records Center. Retrieved from http://www.archives.upenn.edu/people/1800s/taylorjb.html

Phelps, S. & Johnson, M. (1996). *In Contemporary Black Biography,* 13. Detroit, MI: Gale Group.

Rambali,P. (2006). *The Barefoot Runner Barefoot Runner: The Life of Marathon Champion Abebe Bikila.* London, England: Serpents Tail.

Reisler, J. (2012). *Igniting The Flame.* Guilford, Ct: Lyons Press.

Remembering the First U.S. Olympic Team. (n.d). History. Retrieved from http://www.history.com/news/remembering-the-first-u-s-olympic-team

Rosenthal, B. (2000). *Michael Johnson: Sprinter Deluxe,* St. Charles, Mo: GHB Publishers.

Ryun, J. & Phillips, M. (1995). *In Quest of Gold.* Lawrence, KS: Ryun and Sons Publishing.

Sandrock, M. (1996). *Running with the Legends.* Campaign, IL: Human Kinetics.

Schaap, D. (1976). *The Perfect Jump.* New York, NY: New American Library.

Schaap, J. (2007). *Triumph: The Untold Story of Jesse Owens and Hitler's Olympics.* New York: Houghton Mifflin Harcourt.

Schwartz, L. (n.d.). *King Carl Had Long Golden Reign.* Retrieved September 22, 2010 from http://espn.go.com/sportscentury/features/00016079.html

Schul, B., Karuse, L. (2000). *In the Long Run.* Santa Fe, NM: Landfall Press.

Sears, E. (2008). *Running Through The Ages.* Jefferson, NC: McFarland.

Sergey Bubka Official Site. (n.d.). Retrieved September 14, 2010 from www.sergeybubka.com/

Smith, T. and Steele, D. (2007). *Silent Gesture: the autobiography of Tommie Smith,* Philadelphia, PA: Temple University Press.

Tassinm, M. (1983). *Bob Mathias: The Life of the Olympic Champion,* New York, NY: Martin's Press.

Tanber, G. (2008, February 1) Woodruff's forgotten run to Olympic glory. *ESPN*. Retrieved from http://sports.espn.go.com/espn/blackhistory2007/news/story?id=2780877

Team USA. (2012). http://www.teamusa.org/Athletes.aspx

Track and Field News (n.d.) Mountain View, CA: Track and Field News Press.

To Finish the Race: John Stephen Akhwari. (2008, August). Retrieved November 17, 2010 from http://www.gracepointvideo.org/2009/08/to-finish-the-race-john-stephens-akhwari/

USA Track and Field. (n.d.). *Athlete Bios*. www.usatf.org/athletes/bios/

Vorkunov, M. (2012, August 12). Horace Ashenfelter, 1952 Olympic steeplechase champion and FBI agent, never saw himself as a Cold War symbol. *NJ*. Retrieved from http://www.nj.com/olympics/index.ssf/2012/08/horace_ashenfelter_1952_olympi.html

Wallechinsky, D. & Loucky, J. (2008). *The Complete Book of the Olympics, 2008 Edition*. London, England: Aurum Press.

Wheeler, R. (1979). *Jim Thorpe, World's Greatest Athlete*, Norman, OK: University of Oklahoma Press.

Whitfield Foundation. (2010). Retrieved September 21, 2010 form http://www.whitfieldfoundation.org/

Younge. G. (2012, March 30). The man who raised a black power salute at the 1968 Olympic Games. *The Guardian*. Retrieved from http://www.guardian.co.uk/world/2012/mar/30/black-power-salute-1968-olympics

Zirin, D., Carlos, J., & West, C. (2011). *The John Carlos Story, The Sports Moment That Changed the World*. Chicago, Il: Haymarket Books.

About the Author

Dr. Mark Stanbrough is a professor in the Department of Health, Physical Education and Recreation at Emporia State University in Kansas. He teaches graduate and undergraduate exercise physiology and sports psychology classes and is the director of Coaching Education. The Coaching Education program at Emporia State is currently one of only ten universities in the United State to be accredited by the National Council for the Accreditation of Coaching Education. He was a co-founder of the online physical education graduate program, the first in the United States to go completely online. He received his Ph.D. in exercise physiology from the University of Oregon, and undergraduate and master's degrees from Emporia State in physical education. He has served as department chair and has served on the National Association for Sport and Physical Education National Sport Steering Committee and is a past member of the board of directors for the National Council for the Accreditation of Coaching Education.

Mark has over thirty years of coaching experience at the collegiate, high school, middle school and club level. Coach Stanbrough served eight years as the head men's and women's cross country/track and field coach at Emporia State (1984-1992) with the 1986 women's cross country team finishing second at the NAIA national meet. He has also coached at Emporia High School and Glasco High School in Kansas. He is a member of the Emporia State University Athletic Hall of Honor and the Health, Physical Education, Recreation Hall of Honor and has won numerous coach-of-the-year awards at the high school and collegiate levels.